DATE DUE

OCT 01 '97			
MAR 1 8 1998			
FEbR25 2006			
11/2/11			
APR 0 5 2016			
JUN 0 6 2016			

The Mechanics of Judo

The
Mechanics
of
Judo

*Analytical Studies Of
Selected Standing Techniques*

by

Robert G. Blanchard

CHARLES E. TUTTLE COMPANY : PUBLISHERS
Rutland, Vt., & Tokyo, Japan

European Representatives

Continent : BOXERBOOKS, INC., Zurich

British Isles : PRENTICE-HALL INTERNATIONAL INC., London

Published by the
Charles E. Tuttle Company
of Rutland, Vermont & Tokyo, Japan
with editorial offices at
15 Edogawa-cho, Bunkyo-ku, Tokyo

Library of Congress Catalog
Card No. 61–11557
First edition, 1961

Printed in Japan

To
Carol

Table of Contents

List of Illustrations

9

Acknowledgments

A book of this sort owes its existence to many persons, not the least important being all of the judoka with whom an author has had the privilege of practicing. In particular, however, acknowledgment should be made to the following:

To Dewey Lawes Falcone, David H. Massey, and Donald Weimar of Los Angeles who posed for the illustrations.

To Harold Sharp, who made the premises of the Judokan School in North Hollywood available for preparation of pictures.

To Evelyn Hemminger for preparing the manuscript.

To Nanette Schwab for assistance in processing the illustrations.

Most of all, I wish to acknowledge my gratitude to my own teacher. This book will have fulfilled its purpose if it can convey to the reader even a portion of his vast knowledge of both the science and the art of judo.

Introduction

Most books on judo seem to fall naturally into one of two categories —elementary works designed for the beginner or casual reader, and those which seek to give a comprehensive treatment of the whole field. Both are faced with the same problem. It is so difficult at best to make a complex body movement intelligible through the medium of a book that a really adequate description of a given technique will usually confuse the novice rather than assist him. Furthermore, the subject of judo is so large that it is almost impossible to present the whole of it adequately in a single work of reasonable dimensions. Thus, it will be seen that both classes of books are compelled to simplify their treatment of the various techniques to a point which seriously reduces their utility as a means of instruction.

This study will attempt to avoid such a result by seeking a different and more limited objective. Its sole aim will be to increase the student's effectiveness on the mats, and it is addressed primarily to serious judoka who are engaged in regular practice. With this purpose in mind, it is possible to omit many matters of general interest and to present an exhaustive analytical treatment of a limited number of standing techniques. In doing so, emphasis will be placed on the precise way in which the body is to be moved and on the reasons why particular positions and movements are desirable or undesirable. It is hoped in this way to achieve a dual purpose. First, the text will provide a check list for specific points of technique, to be used during practice. Second, it will seek to make the consequences of each variation in style so clear that the student, as he gains experience, will be able to select wisely those forms or modifications most suitable for his own physique and temperament.

The literature of judo describes an infinite number of techniques. Each has certain unique features and any one might be applied successfully in some particular situation. However, this is not to say that they are all of equal worth. Many recognized forms contain intrinsic mechanical weaknesses, so that the time required to master them, while not actually wasted, might be more profitably employed in other directions. Also, a number of techniques once considered highly useful have been supplanted by later developments in the art. Therefore it appears wise to eliminate from this study forms which are less frequently useful, and to include an intensive discussion of the simplest and most effective techniques. The maximum time which the most diligent judoka can devote to practice will hardly suffice to master these few, let alone the variations on them which the text or individual experience will suggest. Moreover, the absolute mastery of even two or three of these forms will often be sufficient to achieve success in contest.

It should of course be self-evident that no single method of performing a given judo technique has an absolute monopoly on correctness for every student under all circumstances. Each experienced judoka will inevitably develop his own individual style, just as each competent instructor will have his own concept of the way in which judo should be studied and performed. The methods recommended in this study represent one such concept. They are not necessarily, in each instance, the easiest to learn. It is believed, however, that once mastered, they will enable most students to achieve maximum effectiveness while employing a minimum of mere physical strength, thereby conforming to the fundamental principle of all good judo.

About the Illustrations

Illustrations in a book of this sort are justified only to the extent that they contribute directly to an understanding of the text. It was soon discovered that this purpose would not be served by using "action" shots, no matter how dramatic or carefully selected they might be. Therefore, each picture has been specially posed to illustrate the form in question.

Even when prepared in this way, it is practically impossible to produce pictures which coincide exactly with every detail recommended in the text. The reader should therefore understand that, in the event of an apparent conflict between some detail of an illustration and the description of the same form, the latter is correct.

Second, it is rarely possible, in a posed picture, to create the dynamic effect of an action shot. Since it has been necessary to sacrifice dynamism for descriptive accuracy, the reader should remember that a given illustration does not necessarily represent the form under discussion just as it would appear in actual contest.

Finally, pictures are meant as a guide, not as a strait jacket. A student who understands and learns to use the basic principles described need not attempt to copy each form down to the last fraction of an inch as it appears in the illustrations.

The Mechanics of Judo

*Strengthen ye the weak hands and
confirm the feeble knees.*

ISAIAH 35:3

1

General Principles of Tachiwaza

In order to absorb the various techniques which are to be described in the pages that follow and to practice them successfully, it is necessary to understand precisely what they are designed to achieve. An analysis of these objectives is therefore in order.

The object of *tachiwaza* is to cause the body of *uke* (the person receiving the attack) to fall cleanly on its back with the minimum expenditure of effort on the part of *tori* (the person attacking). In *tsurikomiashi, hizaguruma* and the forms we will refer to as the rotating techniques, this is done by making uke vault over a portion of tori's body which is employed as a fulcrum. In *ashiharai, okuriashiharai,* and what we will call the advancing techniques, it is achieved by fixing uke's weight on a particular foot or part of a foot and then snatching this support out from under him.

A judoka can achieve these results and thus defeat an opponent of equal or even superior physical strength with a minimum of effort only if he can apply the three basic elements of all *waza:* First, to break his opponent's balance and thereby prevent the latter from effectively exerting his full strength in defense; second, to fit his body and that of his opponent together so that the two form a single functioning unit; and third, to employ the fully coordinated action of all parts of his own body in throwing his opponent to the mat.

Tsukuri is the action of tori's hands and arms which breaks the balance of uke in the direction called for by the particular technique and prepares his body to receive the attack. While all three of the above elements are equally essential if a proper throw is to be achieved, inadequate tsukuri is probably the most frequent cause of failure. To effect proper tsukuri, the following essentials must be observed:

1. The action of the hands must be vigorous. While skilled judoka may occasionally seem to achieve a beautiful-looking throw by delicate hand action, it is impossible to break the balance of a really powerful opponent without an equally powerful tsukuri.

2. The action of the hands must be sudden. A slow pull, no matter how strong, gives the opponent a chance to gather his powers and makes the attempt a mere contest of strength in which the arms invariably come off second best when pitted against the whole body.

We may observe in passing that the arms must be relaxed at all times prior to the commencement of the action. It is impossible to achieve either the speed or the sudden and unexpected action required for successful tsukuri if the muscles of the arms and shoulders are stiff. While the hand grip on opponent's jacket must be reasonably firm, particularly in the little and ring fingers, the muscles of the hands must likewise be relaxed until the instant when the hands are to be used in offensive or defensive action. The weight of the hands and arms should seem to hang gently from the opponent's jacket, thereby creating a delicate contact with the movements of his body and allowing tori to anticipate its action. Ideally, tori should "play" uke through this contact, just as an angler, by a gentle hold on the line, plays a fish which is nibbling at his bait.

3. The action of the hands must be properly timed, neither too soon nor too late in relation to the required movements of the body. Hands and body must coordinate to achieve a successful result and if either acts "out of phase" with the other, the opponent will have ample opportunity to defend or counter before the attack can take effect.

4. The action of the hands must be continuous. An effective initial tsukuri which breaks the opponent's balance is not enough. Unless the pull is maintained and the opponent's balance controlled until the action of body fitting and the final throw are complete, the opponent will be able to recover his balance and may then readily defend or counter.

The principle of fitting the bodies together is the same, whether it involves a complete contact of the back and chest (as in tsurikomi-goshi) or only contact at a single point (as, for example, in hizaguruma). In either case, the throw cannot be completed in proper style unless the two bodies are consolidated into a single piece of machinery with the power unit (tori) firmly linked to the functioning unit (uke). To achieve this efficient mechanical connection, the following conditions must exist:

1.   Tori's body must be in proper posture. Every affirmative movement made in the practice of judo must proceed with the *saika tanden* (lower abdomen) forward, the upper body open with the chest expanded, and (in the initial stages at least) the shoulders relaxed and the head upright. To the degree that the body is jacknifed with the abdomen in and the buttocks out, or the head and shoulders are contracted around a sunken chest, the ability to exert force, either in attack or defense, is reduced. Even though the head, shoulders, and upper body are lowered at the conclusion of many techniques, they must do so over a tanden which remains in a powerful forward position rather than one which falls inward and projects the buttocks outward and the weight back onto the heels. It is not sufficient to achieve a mere superficial resemblance to the real thing by an exaggerated raising of the head and shoulders or an artificial pressing forward of the hips. Proper posture is a matter of effective interior organization of the body which can be achieved only by long and well-disciplined practice.

2.   No matter how vigorous the hand action or how dynamic the movement, tori's body must remain soft. There are several reasons for this. First, tori is required to move swiftly and smoothly into positions of some difficulty if his attack is to succeed. To the extent that his body is hardened and his muscles stiffened, the speed and control necessary for such a movement will be destroyed. Second, it must be remembered that tori's critical objective is not to move himself against uke, but to draw uke's body into contact with his own. A hard, inflexible body will tend to stiffen the muscles of tori's arms and shoulders as well. Tori's hand action thus becomes static rather than dynamic and, despite the fact that it seems to employ a great deal of energy, will communicate little impetus to uke's body. Naturally, the ability to produce the required swift and sudden movement without involuntarily tightening the muscles just before doing so requires long and arduous training.

3.   Tori's movements must be properly timed. As previously indicated, unless body movement and tsukuri commence at the proper time and proceed concurrently in proper relationship to each other, the attempt will not succeed.

4.   Tori's feet must move properly. In fitting the two bodies to-

gether, the feet must slide into position instead of being lifted from the mat. They must remain flat, since rising on the toes will invariably weaken tori's balance and deprive him of the firm foundation necessary for the execution of a throw. However, a flat foot, as the term is used here, is not one in which the weight is carried on the heel, since it is even more fatal to tori's balance if he permits the weight to fall backward. Ideally, tori's feet move with the soles parallel to the ground, but with the weight on the whole forward part of the foot and the heel barely touching the mat, thus achieving both firmness and lightness. Simple as it sounds, this is by no means easy, and it requires long and attentive practice before such a position becomes (as it must) a matter of habit.

When the opponent's balance has been broken and the two bodies locked together, *kake* or the final act of throwing may be performed. The following precautions must be observed in this stage:

1. Kake must employ the whole body as a unit. A frequent cause of failure is to attempt to complete a throw with the strength of the arms or legs alone. Successful kake will result only from the application of the vigorous and expanding power of the body, and primarily that of the hips and tanden. The arms and legs are the means of directing and applying this force but can do nothing unless they are coordinated with it.

2. Kake must be led by the action of the head. As is graphically demonstrated in such sports as diving and tumbling, any movement of the body in a given direction is dependent on the pulling action of the head. If the head remains fixed or moves in a direction opposite to that in which it is intended that the body shall go, the desired action of the body will be slowed down or, in the latter instance, made impossible. Similarly in judo. unless the head is turned or dropped in the direction called for by the completion of the particular technique, the throw will be unsuccessful.

The foregoing remarks have common application to all forms of tachiwaza. While it is impractical to repeat them at length in discussing some particular form, the student should remember that these fundamentals must be read as part of each specific description that follows.

The orthodox classification into *koshiwaza,* or hip techniques, *ashiwaza* or leg techniques, *tewaza* or hand techniques, and so forth, is well known. However, these classes bear no consistent relationship to the type of demand made by them on the body of the person performing the throw. It would seem that a more effective method of classification might be devised which would in itself help the student to understand and remember the basic principles of each form. To this end, the techniques to be described in this study will be presented in the following order:

I.   Six *rotating* techniques in which tori's body turns and presents its back to the opponent, to wit: *Tsurikomigoshi, haraigoshi, hanegoshi, seoinage, uchimata* and *taiotoshi.*

II.   Five *advancing* techniques in which tori's body moves forward against his opponent, to wit: *Osotogari, kosotogari, ouchigari, kouchigari,* and *kouchi-sutemi.*

III.   Four *withdrawing* techniques, in which tori's body moves generally away from or to the side of his opponent without presenting its back to him, to wit: *Ashiharai, okuriashiharai, tsurikomiashi,* and *hizaguruma.*

Before proceeding to a consideration of these forms, one further caution may be useful. Any student of judo may discover that, because of his individual physical or mental makeup, certain recommended positions or movements are particularly difficult for him. As a result, he may wish to adopt for his own use forms which are usually less effective, both in theory and in practice, for most other judoka. This is a reasonable and proper step, and may be beneficial; provided of course that such variations from recommended forms are limited to details which do not destroy the fundamental soundness of his waza. It is important to remember, however, that this is a choice which can only be made intelligently after considerable experience. The forms recommended in this study are those which, from a mechanical viewpoint, appear to promise the best results for most practitioners. A beginning student should persist with them until he has acquired sufficient knowledge to appraise the net gain or loss which may result from the adoption of individualized variants.

2

Tsurikomigoshi

Tsurikomigoshi is the foundation technique of all koshiwaza. For this reason, early and careful study of it is essential to progress. Particular attention should be given to the exhaustive description which follows, since the features which it has in common with other forms will only be referred to briefly hereafter, rather than being again repeated in full.

It is possible to define four distinct forms tsurikomigoshi, any one of which may be found more suitable to the physical conformation of a particular judoka. Because of the many complex movements of different parts of the body which occur simultaneously in tsurikomigoshi, it can be explained most clearly by first describing all of the movements of the feet and then using them as time markers to indicate the actions of the other parts of the body in their proper sequence.

Tsurikomigoshi I

We will first consider the basic or classical form of tusrikomigoshi. Tori's left hand grasps the outside of uke's right sleeve just below the elbow. His right hand takes a full grip on the lapel and front cloth of the jacket somewhat down from the neck at or near the left nipple.

To commence the action, tori's right foot is moved across in front of his body with the foot extended and the leg almost straight to a position about twelve inches in front of uke's right foot and with the toes about on an extension of the inside of that foot (Fig. 1). It is essential, in order to permit the drawing action hereinafter described, that this foot not be placed too close to uke, and a taller judoka may well place it somewhat further away than has been indicated.

Fig. 1. TSURIKOMIGOSHI I. The preparatory action or tsukuri.

Fig. 2. TSURIKOMIGOSHI I. Fitting the bodies together.

When this foot arrives in position, tori's left foot and leg are moved backward in a circular path to a position two or three inches closer to uke than the right foot and just inside the extension of the inside of uke's left foot (Fig. 2). A common fault, especially among beginners, is to place the left foot too far to the front, or to the left, outside of uke's left foot. Either position will prevent tori from achieving the free rotation of his body which makes a successful throw possible. The left foot must come to rest at least parallel with tori's right foot, and preferably slightly closer to uke.

The movement of this foot must be quick, and particularly soft and light. The foot comes to rest at a slight angle outward—that is, aimed somewhat to the left. Both feet slide into position and are not lifted from the mat. The feet remain flat with the weight on the ball and toes. Care should be taken neither to raise the heels from the mat nor to permit the weight to fall back on them.

As the left foot reaches its position, the heel of the right foot rotates outward and the foot turns on the ball until it is pointed slightly to the left and parallel with the left foot (Fig. 3). This turn is essential to permit the hip movement hereinafter described. While these actions follow each other so rapidly as to appear continuous and overlapping, it is helpful to think of them as separate steps, since an attempt to move both feet at once may impair tori's balance.

Most of tori's weight moves onto the right foot in the initial move-

Fig. 3. TSURIKOMIGOSHI I. The throw in progress.

ment. This foot is the foundation of the throw and no appreciable amount of weight is removed from it until the final stage when uke is well on his way to the mat. This placement of weight on the right foot is essential, even though it makes it somewhat more difficult to turn the right heel outward. With sufficient practice, however, the right foot may still be turned adequately. It is moved almost as if it were being screwed forcibly into the mat.

The body follows the initial movement of the right foot with the tanden forward. It is important at this stage that the chest be opened and expanded with the shoulders well back in conformity with the hand action to be described later. The head and shoulders remain upright, but move laterally in conjunction with the lower body so that the head is almost over the right foot as the left foot commences its rotation to the rear. The tanden must remain forward throughout and give the impression that it is leading the hip into position below uke's center of gravity. It is almost impossible to describe this attitude in words, but the correct position is unmistakable when achieved.

As the left foot rotates backward, the body is lowered by bending the knees (with the knees always moving outward, rather than inwards toward each other, in the process) and the right hip moves easily and freely across in front of uke's body to a position about two inches outside his right hip (Fig. 2). This position is essential if the hip is to serve as a fulcrum over which uke's body is to be vaulted. The hip will not be free to complete this movement properly unless the right heel is turned outward as explained above.

Tsurikomigoshi   27

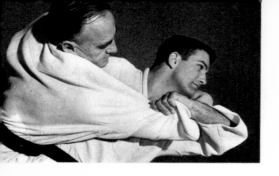

Fig. 4. TSURIKOMIGOSHI I. The left hand action.

It is often difficult to get the hip far enough through, and failure to do so is a common fault. If tori's right hip does not move past that of his opponent, the leverage of the throw is lost, and uke will usually be able to resist with tanden forward, or slide off to his own right. Sometimes a particularly agile and flexible judoka will go to the opposite extreme and get his hip too far through, with the whole right buttock outside his opponent's right thigh, and thereby enable uke to resist or escape by moving to his own left. However, this fault is much less frequent, and most students need have no reservations during practice about attempting to move this hip as far through as seems possible.

While the hips are lowered in this movement, the back remains almost upright with a minimum bending forward at the waist. Care must be taken not to "jackknife" with the tanden in, the buttocks out, and the chest contracted, since this will drive uke backward out of contact and make powerful action by tori difficult unless he possesses physical strength greatly in excess of that of his opponent. As the rotation continues, the upper part of tori's body tends rather to tilt toward his left, exposing his hip and chest for the necessary body contact. Throughout this movement, tori should strive to retain the feeling that his tanden is forward and his weight concentrated in it, even though this may seem difficult when the body is bent to the side and, of necessity, slightly forward. The knees must never be permitted to sag inward, but must be bent slightly outward in order to retain strength and flexibility in the legs.

At an almost imperceptible instant before the initial action of the right foot and body described above, tsukuri is commenced with the hands. The left hand pulls strongly and continuously on uke's right sleeve. Tori's left arm is drawn well up with the elbow raised, ideally just across tori's lower jaw (Fig. 4). The height of the arm may well be exaggerated in practice. The hand and the arm rotate as the pull is

Fig. 5. TSURIKOMIGOSHI I. The right hand action.

made, turning the thumb inward and downward and raising the little finger and the outside of the hand. This assists in keeping the elbow high, produces a straight line of effort from the grip back along a straight wrist and arm, and encourages a strong pull having its foundation in the shoulder and chest muscles.

A slight *outward* feeling in the left hand during the initial stages of the action may assist in opening tori's chest and insuring a good body contact. However, the ultimate direction of the pull is inward, tending to wind uke's right arm closely around tori's open chest, thus welding the two bodies together. In the course of this action the left shoulder moves vigorously backward. A conscious attempt to achieve the impossible here—*i.e.,* to touch the front of the opponent's left shoulder with the back of your own, will help to attain the correct position.

The action of the left hand serves a further purpose. Besides contributing to the breaking of uke's balance, a vigorous pull will force the left shoulder back and open the chest. This action tends to throw the right hip in the opposite direction, thereby making it easier to place this hip properly.

The right hand pulls uke upward and toward tori. To accentuate the open chest and keep the right elbow down, a slight outward pull (toward tori's right) may also be felt in the initial action. As tori's body turns, his right elbow is allowed to bend and his right forearm makes contact with the left front corner of uke's chest below the armpit (Fig. 5). As tori's body turns and tilts to his left, the right arm continues this drawing and lifting action with the length of the forearm firmly against uke's body. This action, together with the continuous pull of the left hand, draws and lifts uke into close contact with tori's chest and hip. Uke is drawn forward onto his toes, and his balance is broken to his right front. The lifting action of tori's right hand is performed with his upper arm close to his tilted body and the forearm almost vertical along a straight line extending from just above his right hip to his grip on uke's jacket.

Beginning students may find that undue emphasis on the right-hand action will sometimes tend to raise the right elbow, close the chest, and collapse the waist inward, thereby reducing the effectiveness of the whole action. When first studying this technique, it may be helpful to concentrate only on keeping the right hand well back with the elbow down and the forearm vertical rather than seeking to exert maximum force with it. If this is done while the left-hand pull is properly maintained, it is probable that the correct lift-pull action with the right will occur almost automatically as the body rotates with the chest opened, the body tilted, and the knees bent.

As more familiarity with the movement is gained and the student is able to conform consistently with the proper pattern of open chest and high left hand, more force may be applied with the right, driving always upward rather than in a circular path around tori's hips. Although a contrary opinion is frequently expressed, a powerful right-hand action, *if correctly performed,* is of equal or even greater importance than the left in attaining success. The criteria of correct use of the right hand are: (1) that it is directed upward with the forearm vertical and the elbow down; and (2) that it does not impair the expanded chest or the forward position of the abdomen.

It is essential to any successful waza that the tsukuri commence first; that the body movement start *immediately* afterward (the difference in time being almost imperceptible); and that both hand and body action continue thereafter without interruption. If hand action is delayed until the body is committed to the throw, uke's balance will not be broken and he can readily defend or counter. Conversely, if the arms act too far in advance of the body, a lapse in control over the opponent may occur while the body is catching up to the action, and uke may be able to recover his balance.

It is likewise essential that the pull be *maintained* throughout the throw. If tori loses hand control, even for an instant during the course of the movement, his opponent may escape, no matter how successful the initial pull may have been in achieving a temporary breaking of balance.

The opening of the chest, the withdrawing of the left shoulder, and the tilting of tori's body all contribute to the maintenance of continuous tsukuri. Failure in any one of these respects may cause the necessary contact and control to be lost.

We have already seen that the intial action of the hands must be sharp and sudden if uke's balance is to be broken properly. A slow pull, no matter how much strength is employed, will never produce a well-executed throw, nor indeed any throw at all, except against a weaker opponent. Many judoka have difficulty in combining this quick muscular reaction with the continued pull which is also necessary. The following device may be found useful to meet the problem.

Even though the purpose of the hand action in a given technique may be to break uke's balance upward, the initial impact of the hands may be directed downward. This action is not a continued pull, but only a quick snatch, felt principally in the heels of tori's hands and the little and ring fingers, which merges instantly into the direction called for by the particular technique. If properly executed, this downward movement is so swift as to be practically invisible to the spectator, and uke may not even realize just what has taken place. Trivial as it may seem, however, this action is extremely effective. It draws uke's weight forward on his toes, and the sudden shock imparted to his head and neck may destroy his concentration for the instant which is necessary to complete the throw. Tori must take care not to "wind up" with his hands, but, from a position with the hands in repose, should pull suddenly and without warning.

The placement of the feet may also have a significant effect in connection with proper tsukuri. Unless the initial movement of tori's left hand actually takes control of uke's right side and starts his weight moving forward and upward, uke may be warned in time to withdraw his arm from the impending attack. If tori's right foot is advanced too close to uke's body (the precise distance depending to some degree on the relative height and arm length of the contestants) uke may absorb the first few inches of pull in his arm without permitting his body balance to be affected. This instant of relative freedom may well permit uke to establish a successful defense. If, on the other hand, tori moves to a position far enough in front of uke, the first movement of his left hand is more likely to have an instantaneous effect on balance and thus greatly adds to tori's chances of success.

The final impetus of the throw is achieved by the movement of tori's head which turns sharply to the left. The chin does not drop to the chest but rotates toward the left shoulder, causing the head to tilt in the same manner as the body and imparting a noticeable stretching to the muscles in the right side of the neck (Fig. 3). A natural reluctance to lose sight of one's opponent causes many judoka to slight this turn of the head. This will block the free turning of the body and is a frequent cause of failure. Self-deception is easy on this point, and many judoka unconsciously continue to watch their opponent or their own form out of a corner of the eye while honestly believing that the head has been adequately turned. It is often beneficial to concentrate on the turn of the head during practice, even commencing the move sooner than is absolutely necessary.

If tori's body has been properly lowered; if his chest has been well opened; and if the action of both hands has been properly applied and maintained, uke's balance will have been broken to his right front, and his body will have been loaded on that of tori, with a tight contact extending down the side of tori's chest and the back of his hip and his right arm drawn firmly across and against the front of tori's chest. The continuation of the pull of tori's left hand, *the upward drive of his right hand,* and the tilting and turning of his body, led by the action of his head, will rotate uke's body over and around tori's hip and drop it to the mat in front of and slightly to tori's left.

The efficiency of this technique may be greatly enhanced by a proper movement of the right knee. It will be recalled that the knees must always be bowed slightly outward, and that any tendency toward a "knock-kneed" stance is extremely weak. Thus, tori's right knee must remain slightly outside his right foot at all times.

However tori, at the instant of kake as his right heel rotates outward in the manner previously described, should move his right knee forward, downward and inward, traveling in a small circular path around the outside of the foot position (Fig. 3). This is a relatively slight movement, and should never proceed so far as to deprive the leg of strength and balance, as would be the case if tori were actually preparing to kneel down. However, the consequences of this action are substantial.

This action of the knee causes tori's right hip and side to be slightly lowered. This has a twofold effect: (1) it eliminates the possibility that tori's hip may be raised and block the normal movement of the throw; and (2) it adds the force of gravity to the pull of tori's hands. Uke's body, which has been drawn onto tori's hip and side, can thus be thrown to the mat with greater speed and ease.

This matter of lowering the right hip deserves further consideration since a proper appreciation of the point is essential to success against a strong opponent. The function of the hip is to serve as a fulcrum over which uke is turned. If tori's waist slants upward from uke's left to his right, tori is compelled to employ increased muscular effort to lift uke over the raised right hip. He must often straighten his legs and lift the hip even higher in an effort to hoist uke with the buttocks. Such an effort relies on strength rather than skill and contradicts the basic principles of good judo. A throw will usually be achieved in this way only against a physically weaker or less experienced opponent, and, even though it succeeds, may be properly viewed as *muri* or "unreasonable."

If, on the other hand, tori strives to keep his hips as much as possible on a constant level from the commencement of the throw, and finally to arrive at the point of kake with the right hip lower than the left, an entirely different condition results. There is no violent impact between the two bodies. Nothing interferes with tori's hand action which then causes uke's body to flow smoothly forward toward the fulcrum. Complete body contact is readily achieved and uke's body is brought to a state of maximum instability. The proposition that the hips should always be lowered rather than raised, with the leading hip lowered to a proportionately greater degree, is an axiom of almost universal application to the rotating techniques recommended in this work, and, to a substantial degree, will apply to other techniques as well.

Obviously the proper use of this device presupposes that tori's hips have been moved well through and that his tsukuri has been effective in controlling uke's movements and achieving a firm body contact. If this has not been done, the final lowering of the knee and hip might permit uke to slide off to his own right. It is thus sometimes wise not to overemphasize the terminal action of right hip and knee in practice until the basic patterns of hand and body movement are well established. However, if the prior steps of the form have been proper and the hips have remained substantially on a level, the ultimate lowering of the knee will enable tori to complete the throw with maximum speed and a minimum of effort. Since the muscular strain required is thus reduced, tori's ability to maintain perfect balance and body control is improved; his performance becomes more consistent; and the dangers of being countered are lessened.

While the lowering of the body is of course essential in this as well as all other rotating techniques, a frequent defect is not the failure to lower the body at all, but that it is lowered improperly—*i.e.,* with the abdomen jackknifed and the chest collapsed. For this reason, an effective method of practice is to perform uchikomi with the body remaining almost straight upright, concentrating on keeping the tanden forward, the hip well through, the chest opened, and the left arm and shoulder drawn well back. When this position is well established by frequent repetitions, the body can gradually be lowered by bending the knees without danger of relapsing into an incorrect position. In uchikomi it is well to drop even lower than usual, in order that a normal correct position will more easily be achieved when the throw is attempted in the stress of randori or contest.

As has been indicated, tori must always keep the left hand high, turn the chin rather than drop the head downward, and maintain the left-hand pull well across the open chest with the left shoulder withdrawn. This attitude of the hand, head, and chest is the hallmark of the koshiwaza techniques described in this study. When they have been impressed on the muscle memory, they produce an ideal co-ordination of the left shoulder and right hip which seem to move *against* each other around a solid tanden. The shoulder draws strongly to the left while the right hip moves with machine-like precision to the right, below and outside of uke's waist.

Before concluding this extended discussion of the most funda-mental of the rotating techniques, it may be well to emphasize again the transcendent importance of a powerful and effective tsukuri. This point is sometimes graphically demonstrated by a judoka who is an extremely dangerous and successful contestant, despite his ob-vious lack of what is usually accepted as good form. Invariably such a result may be attributed to his powerful tsukuri, and demonstrates that in contest it is better to have a strong pull and no form than perfect form and no pull.

Of course, no intelligent judoka will take this advice literally, and use it as an excuse to avoid the effort required for the acquisition of good style. It should be obvious that one who combines good tech-niques with a powerful pull will almost always defeat an opponent who lacks either the one or the other. If, however, successful throws do not seem to be coming as easily or as frequently as they should, the most effective immediate remedy will usually be to relax the body and to pull quicker and harder with the hands.

Fig. 6. TSURIKOMIGOSHI II. Tori's left arm is somewhat lowered to reveal the proper right arm position.

Tsurikomigoshi II

A second variant form of tsurikomigoshi is particularly suitable for shorter judoka, or for those who have stiffness in the shoulders. A naturally right-handed judoka may sometimes find this form more comfortable for use on his left side, and vice versa.

This form starts in the same manner as before. However, the bending of the knees is greatly increased. It is desirable to lower the hips as far as is physically possible without destroying the ability of the legs to retain balance and to respond quickly to the need for further movement. The placement of the right arm is altered, with the forearm being placed against the center of the chest instead of below the armpit (Fig. 6). Thus tsukuri with the right hand tends to displace uke's balance upward and forward rather than to the right front, as in the classical form. The right forearm still lies in an upright position extending from tori's right hip, somewhat in the manner of a weight-lifter performing a bent-press lift. The right hand is relatively more important in this technique, and its placement and vigorous action, combined with the lowering of the body, loads uke's body higher on tori's back.

The action of the left hand here is in a more downward direction. However, it is lower only in relation to uke's body (because of tori's bent knees). As far as tori is concerned, it remains high, crossing his body, as usual, well up toward his chin.

Tsurikomigoshi   35

FIG. 7. TSURIKOMIGOSHI III. Uke's body drawn upward into contact.

In kake, the lowering of tori's right knee, which has been previously described, is somewhat more pronounced. The path of uke's body is somewhat more in a vertical plane over the hip and less of a rotation around it. He usually falls to the mat directly in front of tori rather than somewhat to his left front, as in the classical form.

Tsurikomigoshi III

Another form of tsurikomigoshi is often suitable for taller judoka or for those who have difficulty in bending the knees.

In this form, the feet move in a similar manner to the classical form, but are placed much closer to uke. The heels of tori's feet in their final position should be about level with and just inside uke's toes. The body remains entirely upright with only a slight bending at the knees.

While tori's left hand grasps the sleeve in the usual manner, his right hand is placed at the back of uke's collar. As the right foot commences its movement, tori's right arm embraces uke's head and neck. The hand may either remain on the collar (thus obtaining a certain amount of lift from tension on the jacket) or may release this grip and reach further around the head. In either event, the hugging action of this arm, together with the upward pull of the left hand in the usual manner, breaks uke's balance and produces a complete body contact between the two bodies from the hips upward. If properly executed, uke will be drawn up on his toes and his body will be held in an upright position (Fig. 7).

Fig. 8. TSURIKOMIGOSHI III. Uke's body lifted up for the throw.

As tori's right heel rotates outward in the usual manner, he tilts his body strongly to his left front and springs slightly upward by straightening the knees and even by rising somewhat on the toes (Fig. 8). Uke, who is already locked against tori's back, will be rolled easily across his hip and thrown directly to the front.

Care should be taken not to rotate the shoulders in kake. Such a forward movement of tori's right shoulder will tend to throw uke's body outward, and make the success of the throw dependent almost entirely upon mere strength of arm, rather than upon the coordinated action of the whole body. Tori's body must tilt forward and to his left with the chest open, much as in the classical form (although it will in all probability not move quite so far to the left as in the usual style).

It will be observed that the close-in position of tori's feet seriously limits his ability to draw uke's body forward onto his hip with the kind of tsukuri employed in the other hip techniques described in this study. From a close position, tori's own body may sometimes assist uke in defending. This departure from standard practice may be used here only because tori's body remains fully upright until a complete body contact has been attained by the action of the right arm and left hand. Once the two bodies are locked together in this position, tori can straighten his knees and tilt his upper body into the throw without danger of losing control.

A student who attempts this style of tsurikomigoshi before he has firmly established the movement patterns of the orthodox form may

Tsurikomigoshi   37

Fig. 9. TSURIKOMIGOSHI III. Another method of using the right hand.

seriously hamper his future progress in the art. He should therefore resist the temptation to practice it too soon, even though it may seem less physically exacting and may produce a few early successes. However, an experienced judoka may find this form extremely useful when faced with an opponent of the same or shorter stature who possesses a strong upright defensive posture. It is particularly helpful against a strong but obese type, who is built low to the ground and carries his tanden well forward.

This technique, most frequently employed by tall men, suggests a variation in the use of the right hand which may be applied to other rotating forms. We have already described the normal use of this hand, involving a grip near uke's left nipple and an upward thrust with the vertical forearm against his chest. A taller judoka will naturally tend to grip higher up on the jacket. If, however, this difference in height is substantial, tori may find it extremely awkward to lower his body sufficiently to utilize the orthodox form.

In this event, he may compromise by gripping the jacket at the side of or even behind the neck, and drawing directly forward with the right hand. As this occurs, tori's right arm bends at the elbow, which is raised to the side to a position more or less on a level with the hand (Fig. 9). This drawing action will produce the full body contact which is essential and will facilitate a successful throw. Of course, the benefits of the upward-driving right hand which are present in the orthodox form are lost, and more of the responsibility for completion of the throw must be assumed by the left. Tori is almost sure to destroy his balance and lose the proper body position *(i.e.,* to collapse his chest and waist) if, having once raised the elbow in this way, he then attempts to power his opponent to the ground with the right hand. However, if employed with discretion as a means of procuring and retaining body contact, this method will produce a net profit for the taller judoka.

Fig. 10. SODE-TSURIKOMIGOSHI. The grip with the right hand.

Some readers may remark on the absence from this work of a detailed description of ukigoshi or ogoshi, forms frequently described elsewhere. These throws are similar in principle to that method of tsurikomigoshi just described, but different in the following respects:

1. Tori's body is placed somewhat lower by bending the knees.

2. His right arm is inserted around uke's waist, with the hand grasping the back of the jacket or belt.

Ukigoshi and ogoshi may be quite powerful especially for the shorter judoka and the details of their execution are somewhat less complex than other forms. However, it is extremely difficult to succeed in inserting the right arm deeply around the waist of a really capable opponent. Unless this can be done quickly and completely, the throw will not succeed and thus it is rarely attempted in competition by experienced judoka.

Ukigoshi and ogoshi are most useful as counters after uke has put his body into a position which makes this arm placement easier. In general, however, practice time devoted to them would appear to be less rewarding than if it were employed on other and more effective forms.

Sode-tsurikomigoshi

A fourth form of this technique, particularly suitable for shorter judoka, is sode-tsurikomigoshi, or the sleeve technique.

The movement of the feet and body in sode-tsurikomigoshi is

Fig. 11. SODE-TSURIKOMIGOSHI. The action of the right hand and arm.

comparable to that of the orthodox forms described, except that tori's right hip moves further out past that of uke, preferably extending from six to eight inches. The principal distinction is found in the action of the hands.

The right hand of tori grasps the inside of uke's left sleeve at the middle of the forearm. The fingers take a generous fold of the sleeve with the thumb rotated outward and the palm somewhat up (Fig. 10). The left hand may retain the usual grip but it is preferable to grasp the inside of uke's sleeve in the same manner as the right.

With the initial move of the foot and body, the right hand draws uke's left arm slightly inward. It then lifts strongly upward, raising uke's left arm high in the air. Tori's right forearm is placed against the underside of uke's upper arm and his elbow inserted in the armpit (Fig. 11). When combined with the usual pulling action of the left hand, this breaks uke's balance upward and to his right.

As this action continues, a rotating movement is imparted to uke's body by the lifting of his left arm and the downward and forward tension on his right. At the moment of kake, tori's right knee is lowered, as previously described, and uke's body is cast vigorously forward with a whirling motion and strikes the mat to tori's right front.

This casting of uke's body outward, to the right front, is a distinctive feature of the form, since, in all other koshiwaza, uke's body falls to tori's front or left front. In sode-tsurikomigoshi, the head drops forward at the time of kake, in the same general direction as that in which uke's body is thrown, and the rotation of the chin to tori's left is somewhat less pronounced.

The key to successful completion of this technique is the placement of tori's right elbow at uke's armpit. This contact imparts a vigor to the effort which is lost if tori's right hand on the sleeve is the sole point of connection. Care must be taken not to grip the top or outside of uke's right sleeve. If this is done, the upward drive of tori's right arm tends to pull the fingers loose from their grip on the sleeve. With the inside grip above described, tori's fist is pressed against the underside of uke's arm as it is raised. This adds force to the action and relieves pressure on the finger grip which is held even tighter by the weight bearing downward on the knuckles.

Sode-tsurikomigoshi is not an easy form to bring off, since it requires great strength and skill to force an opponent's right arm up into the required position. Generally speaking, it should be attempted only by judoka of relatively short stature who, for this reason, are usually in a better position to exert leverage under a taller antagonist's arm. It may sometimes be particularly useful to one who normally assumes the right-hand position *(i.e.,* with his right hand at the collar and left hand on the sleeve), but who is able to lift his opponent's right arm in the air and attack in the opposite direction without changing his usual handgrip.

3

Hanegoshi

Hanegoshi is identical with the classical form of tsurikomigoshi up to the point at which the body has turned into position with the hip well through, the left foot has arrived in its proper position, and tsukuri has been correctly performed with the chest well open, breaking uke's balance to his right front, and producing a firm contact between the two bodies.

As the feet arrive at their proper positions, however, the right foot is raised so as to be barely in contact with the mat but free of all weight. The toe is pointed; the knee out, extending past uke's right leg; the sole of the foot inward (*i.e.,* toward the left); and the top of tori's extended foot placed along the inside of uke's right leg just at the ankle (Fig. 12). The contact must *never* be made with the toes curled up rather than pronated and with the outer edge of the foot rather than the top against uke's leg, since this will reduce tori's ability to control uke's leg, and will cause unnecessary pain to both parties. It is mechanically impossible for tori to assume the correct position unless his knee is moved to the outside of uke's leg. In the traditional method once common, the contact was made with tori's knee bent and his lower leg raised across uke's upper thigh, but this method has proved much less successful and requires the employment of excessive physical strength.

From the position described, tori's right leg is moved strongly to his rear, carrying uke's right leg in the same direction. While tori's knee remains outside uke's leg, the movement is primarily to the rear with little if any displacement to the right (Fig. 13). If tori's leg moves too much to the side, it will tend to tilt his whole body directly to his left instead of to his left front. If this occurs, tori loses body contact,

43

Fig. 12. HANEGOSHI. The initial position of the right foot and leg.

Fig. 13. HANEGOSHI. The start of the leg action.

balance, and much of the benefit of his tsukuri. Tori's action cannot be taken with the leg alone, but must arise from a vigorous springing action in the right thigh and hip, hinged at his left hip and counterbalanced by the whole action of the upper body.

Concurrently with the movement of the leg described above, kake is performed in a manner similar to tsurikomigoshi. The chin rotates to the left shoulder, the hands continue a strong lifting and pulling action, and the body tilts well to the left front. The head and upper body will tilt forward toward the ground, to or even past a horizontal position, as the right leg moves back and up (Fig. 14). The action may be likened to that of a single span drawbridge in which the head and upper body form the counterweight, the left leg the main pier, the left hip the hinge, and the right leg the moving roadway. The action has much in common with uchimata.

Care must be taken that the pivot area, the hips and abdomen, remain relatively "forward," that is, in substantially the same relationship to the original vertical axis of the body as at the start of the throw. Proper performance of the technique will be prevented if the body jackknifes inward at the waist, moving the buttocks backward against uke.

Of course, the proper lowering of the hips requires the bending of the left knee. As the knee is bent, care must be taken that the weight

Fig. 14. HANEGOSHI. Completing the throw.

remains well balanced on the ball of the foot and that the muscles
of the foot and knee are controlled and flexible like steel springs. The
placement of the weight on this foot must achieve a precise happy
median between instability, which results if the balance is too far
toward the toes, and rigidity, which follows if it is allowed to fall back
on the heel. The latter fault is particularly destructive, since it tends
to collapse the weight inward and to stiffen all of the muscles of the
body.

The effect of the action of the right leg is to raise the whole of uke's
right leg backward and finally to a position almost parallel with the
ground, thereby removing all support from the right side of his body.
The continuing action of the hands will therefore readily rotate uke
over tori's right hip and upper thigh, dropping his body to the mat.

The power of the leg is not the really crucial factor in this form as
might seem to be the case at first glance. Success here is dependent
on the effective action of the hands and particularly the left hand. If
uke's balance is properly broken and his body controlled by tori's
hand action, uke's stability will be so thoroughly disturbed that his
body will seem to float and a relatively gentle stroke of the leg will
complete the throw. If, however, tori's hands do not do an adequate
job, the throw will not succeed, no matter how powerful his leg action
may be. As a matter of fact, if tori tightens up the muscles of the leg
and body in an attempt to produce a powerful impact, this will in
itself cut short any continued pull of the hands, and achieve precisely

Hanegoshi 45

the opposite result from that which he is seeking. Like all koshiwaza forms, hanegoshi uses the hip as a fulcrum over which uke is thrown. Even though the hip is correctly moved well to the outside, this fulcrum may be destroyed and the throw blocked if the hip is lifted rather than being retained at a constant level. Therefore, it is a serious fault for tori to *lift* his right leg either to the rear or to the outside, since this will inevitably raise his hip as well.

The action of this leg is not a lifting but rather a *thrusting* to the rear. The foot remains low as long as possible with the toes almost touching the mat. The right knee drops toward the ground as the leg is thrust backward, and the leg will not rise appreciably until uke is in the process of being projected over tori's hip and the throw is for all practical purposes achieved. Of course, the foot and leg may ultimately rise almost to the level of the hip, but this occurs too late to interfere with its proper function as a fulcrum. As a matter of fact, the dropping of the knee can cause the right hip and thigh to be actually lowered after uke's body has been drawn into contact. This lowering of the hip makes it much easier for uke's body to drop over it, much in the manner of the tsurikomigoshi form which has been already described. It causes uke's body to fall somewhat more to tori's front rather than around his body to the left front, and greatly reduces the amount of muscular effort required in the throw. The best way to really master this method is to concentrate on practice of tsurikomigoshi, with emphasis on the lowering of the right knee and hip. Once the feeling of this form has been digested, it is relatively easy to achieve a comparable hanegoshi and to avoid the raising of the right hip which is the most common cause of failure.

It will be observed that the form described above involves an approach well in front of uke's original position and requires that uke be drawn forward to achieve the proper breaking of balance and body contact. The following variation may be found more comfortable, particularly by shorter judoka.

In this method, tori moves well in against uke's body, placing his right toes about level with those of uke. The knees are bent as deeply as possible and the hips lowered. The action of the hands is similar to the Tsurikomigoshi II and tends to move uke less to his right but more upward on tori's back. Failure to get low enough is fatal to this form since the close position will tend to support uke's balance against the action of tori's hands unless it is possible to pull him over tori's lowered body.

As tori's leg moves to the rear, the lowering of the right knee and hip, in the manner already described, is particularly pronounced and tori's right-hand action is somewhat more significant. The throw concludes much in the same fashion as Tsurikomigoshi II, with uke's body moving more in a vertical plane rather than around the hip and thigh, and falling somewhat more to tori's right than usual.

4

Haraigoshi

The orthodox form of haraigoshi is commenced in the same manner as tsurikomigoshi, with the identical tsurikomi or lift-pull. The two techniques proceed in a substantially similar way up to the point at which both feet are in their final position parallel to each other; tori's hip has moved through and to the outside of uke's; tsukuri with both hands is well in effect; the chest is open and the left shoulder well back; and a firm contact is established with uke's body along the full length of tori's hip and the right rear corner of his chest. In haraigoshi, tori may move somewhat closer to uke, with his upper body not tilted quite so much to his left and his hip not quite so far through. The final position of his left foot may be somewhat farther to uke's right: that is, approaching a line drawn through the mid-point between uke's feet rather than one extended from the inside of his left foot. However, these details are matters of degree which cannot be specifically defined and each judoka must arrive by feel at the pattern most suited to his own physique.

At this point, tori's right leg, with the toe pointed and the leg almost straight *(i.e.,* flexed at the knee only enough to prevent stiffness), is raised to tori's right front with the toes pointed and swept smoothly backward, upward, and inward in a circular path (Fig. 15). As the leg strikes, kake is performed in a manner similar to tsurikomigoshi. Tori's head rotates to his left, the body strongly follows the action of the head with the left shoulder well back, and tension with both hands is strongly maintained (Fig. 16). Uke's balance has already been broken to his right front. His legs are swept out of contact with the ground, his body is whirled over tori's thigh, and he is thrown to the mat at tori's right front (Fig. 17).

Fig. 15. HARAIGOSHI. Commencing the leg movement.

Fig. 16. HARAIGOSHI. The leg sweep in progress.

A useful training device is to hesitate for an instant just before the
leg action is commenced; then to raise the right leg with the toe
pointed forward, much in the manner of osotogari; and to swing it
to the rear and upward with a somewhat exaggerated circular action.
Of course, this cannot be done in randori or contest, but if occasionally
used in uchikomi it will give the student a feeling for the smooth,
full action of the leg that is desired, and prevent him from merely
stabbing his leg backward against uke's ankle or knee in a constrained
and jerky manner.

There is a considerable difference of opinion as to the most desirable
point on uke's right leg at which the first contact should be made.
Some experts swing the leg high, making contact with the underside
of the thigh against the outside of uke's upper thigh. Force is applied
both upward and inward. In this form, tori must take particular
care to keep his left knee bent and not to rise on the toes of the left
foot. Failure in these respects tends to raise tori's hips, making it easier
for uke to resist and requiring a much greater expenditure of strength
and effort if the throw is to be completed. It is essential that tori's
hips remain at a constant level below uke's waist, no matter how his
leg is used.

Other highly competent judoka suggest that the first contact be
made lower on the leg, even as far down as the calf. From this point

Fig. 17. HARAIGOSHI. Completing the throw.

tori's leg slides upward *and inward* along the outside of uke's leg and pressures it out from under him. The effectiveness of this style is increased if the inward movement of tori's leg (that is, to tori's left and under uke's right hip) is made more pronounced than usual.

Neither of these two methods appears to have a pronounced intrinsic advantage over the other. As a matter of fact, close study would indicate that they do not differ as fundamentally as might appear at first glance.

The key points to success in haraigoshi are: (1) a strong and continuous pull, particularly with the left hand; (2) the achievement of complete body contact, with uke's body drawn well forward onto tori's hip; and (3) a smooth, well-controlled circular sweep of the leg. If the first two points are achieved, power in the leg is of secondary importance, and, when a high degree of skill has been achieved, the leg will remain relatively soft throughout.

A jukoka who performs haraigoshi with his right hip well through past uke's and his right foot placed initially on an extension of uke's right foot is more likely to swing his leg high, particularly if he is relatively taller than his opponent. On the other hand, if his right foot moves initially to a point inside uke's right foot, and his right hip is barely past or even falls short of his opponent's, a contact lower on the leg would naturally follow, especially if tori is the shorter of the two contestants.

Each student may decide for himself which method seems most congenial. However, the differences between the two forms are more

Fig. 18. HARAIGOSHI II. The initial body turn and leg entry.

superficial than fundamental and it is not really necessary to make a calculated election between them, it being sufficient to concentrate on the more vital elements of the throw, and make leg contact in the most effective way that can be achieved in each particular situation which may be presented during contest.

If the essential requirements of tsukuri, body contact, and smooth leg sweep are observed, numerous variations in the placement of the hands may be adopted to suit individual preference. The right hand may be placed at the back of the collar, around uke's head, or passed under uke's left arm and placed against his back. Many experts prefer to put both hands on the opponent's lapels. Some even find it effective to insert the right arm through and under uke's *right* armpit in the manner of ipponseoinage. Care must be taken that, in adopting any of these variation from the normal style, the basic essentials of successful koshiwaza are not neglected. If tori permits his attention to wander from the need for the vigorous pull, the open chest, and the forward tanden, the throw will fail no matter what position of the hands is used.

Haraigoshi II

After having achieved a degree of skill with this form, it is possible to increase one's chances of success in contest by the following variation. Instead of advancing his right foot and withdrawing his left in the usual way, tori's first action is to rotate his body and hips in a

Fig. 19. HARAIGOSHI II. Moving into the throw. Arrows indicate the rotation of feet and hips.

counterclockwise direction and pivot on the ball of his left foot. As he does so, his right leg is threaded through the opening between the two bodies and raised outside of uke's right leg without again touching the mat (Fig. 18). The toe is pointed and the leg almost straight, much like the initial action in osotogari. As his body continues to rotate, the right leg sweeps back in a circular path with the toes turned down and strikes against uke's right leg (Fig. 19). The actions of hand, chest, shoulders, and head are the same as in the orthodox form and the left leg ultimately assumes the same posture, with the knee bent and the foot turned slightly to tori's left.

It will be observed that, by combining two separate movements into one, this form develops more rapidly than the usual method and will thus be more effective in contest. However, it is proportionately more difficult to perform, requiring great ability, superior body control, and a highly developed power to apply and maintain tsukuri. It is thus recommended only for experienced and skillful practitioners.

In one respect, however, some judoka may find this form less taxing than the normal method. It will be recalled that a common error in the performance of all hip techniques is to place the left foot outside of the opponent's. Unless tori is able to rotate in a relatively small, compact circle so that his left foot comes to rest parallel with his right and inside the extension of uke's left foot, he will rarely succeed with koshiwaza.

However, tori may first maneuver his own left foot to a position

Haraigoshi   53

slightly to uke's right, and outside of the latter's right foot. If, from this position, he pivots on it and attacks in the manner just described, he will find that, as the throw is completed, his left foot falls more easily into the correct position in relation to uke's feet. With his left foot thus well to the inside, his ability to maintain proper balance and complete the throw in good style is greatly enhanced. The method is still not one for the novice; but a judoka who has acquired some skill may find it easier to master this difficult body turn than to get his left foot into the proper position by the orthodox method.

One particular problem which arises in using this form requires special mention. In studying other hip techniques we find that much of tori's weight must move onto his right foot as it is advanced into position, and must remain on that side until the throw is practically complete. If this is not done, tori will fall off balance to his left and can succeed neither in completing the throw nor avoiding a counter. This is equally true in this variant of haraigoshi. Tori's body weight must be moved and controlled just as if his right foot were advanced in the usual way and had remained on the ground until his left foot arrived at its final position. Therefore, tori must guard against a strong tendency to let the weight remain on the left foot while the right leg reaches away from it toward uke's side. This will almost guarantee a fatal loss of balance. At first glance it might seem impossible for tori to move his weight to the right without falling down if there is no foot to support it. However, if his hand action is proper, uke's body serves as a counterweight to preserve tori's balance until the throw is well on its way to completion.

Some judoka will advance the left foot slightly in a feint at uke's right ankle, and place it on the ground with the toes turned somewhat to the left before starting to attack with haraigoshi. Others will move the left foot well across in front of uke's body, much as if commencing tsurikomigoshi to the opposite side. Such actions have a certain value in deceiving the opponent and some judoka may find the particular rhythm of the movement congenial. It is believed, however, that anything more than a slight feint will produce a net loss of efficiency rather than a gain, since this will require even more agility and coordination than the variant described above, but affords no saving in time over the orthodox method.

5

Seoinage

Seoinage or shoulder throw is often applied without much discrimination to either of two distinct forms which can be more specifically identified by proper usage. We shall first describe that which is properly named *ipponseoinage* or one-arm shoulder throw, which is often abbreviated to *ipponseoi*.

Ipponseoinage

The first caution to be observed in ipponseoi is to place the left hand, not on the sleeve as usual, but on the right side of uke's collar, reaching *over* his right arm. This is desirable because it permits tori to lock uke's right arm in the course of the throw. Unless this is done, uke can readily use his right arm to strangle tori or at least to unbalance him to his rear and thus frustrate the attempt.

Those who have a strong preference for a grip on the sleeve should move their handhold somewhat onto the top of uke's right forearm rather than the side so as to obtain some protection against this danger. It may be observed in passing that familiarity with the collar grip in ipponseonage may be turned to advantage by one who can make such an attack to the left without reversing his normal hand position.

Tori first advances his right foot across in front of uke's body, placing the toes in a position approximately two inches inside and in front of the toes of uke's right foot (Fig. 20). The left foot then rotates backward in the usual fashion to a position inside of and approximately level with uke's right foot. The body turns, following the movement of the feet, and the hip is inserted approximately two inches past uke's right hip. The body remains upright but the knees are bent

Fig. 20. IPPONSEOINAGE. The initial action.

Fig. 21. IPPONSEOINAGE. Completing the body contact.

and the hips lowered sufficiently to permit proper arm action—the precise point to which the body must be lowered depending on the relative height of the two contestants (Fig. 21).

Simultaneously with the commencement of the first foot movement, tori's left hand draws uke upward and forward. It will be observed that, as tori's body continues to rotate and the pull of his left hand is maintained with the elbow bent, it tends to lock uke's right arm between tori's left forearm and chest.

At the same time, tori's right hand releases its grip on uke's left lapel and drops downward until the hand is in the area of tori's right hip or thigh with the arm slightly bent. Then, as the hip moves across in front of uke's body, the hand and arm follow it, swinging in an upward arc, and are inserted under uke's right arm and through below the armpit (Fig. 20). Care must be taken that this arm movement coincides with the movement of the hip. If done too soon, it may interfere with the turn of the hip while, conversely, the arm can be blocked by the hip if it moves too late. The arm is inserted with a vigorous swinging motion and is raised until it makes contact with uke's armpit just about at the junction of the deltoid and bicep muscles (Fig. 21). It is erroneous to permit the contact to be made either low near the elbow or high over the deltoid muscle. As the arm is inserted, tori's elbow is bent and his hand moves toward his own

Fig. 22. IPPONSEOINAGE. Ready to complete the throw.

shoulder until it is almost above the point of contact between the two arms. The forearm remains upright, however, and it is both awkward and unnecessary to seek a grip with the right hand on uke's jacket as is sometimes suggested. The right forearm is tilted a little backward, thus causing tori's whole upper body to lean slightly toward uke, with the chest particularly well open. This movement can, of course, be carried to extremes, in which event tori may well lose his balance to the rear when uke resists. However, the proper amount of backward lean, combined with the lowering of the hips in the correct degree will concentrate the whole power of tori's waist and back under the shoulders at the point where the two bodies are joined. Each judoka must determine for himself the proper combination of these elements, depending on his own physical conformation and the relative height of the contestants. Generally speaking, of course, seoinage is always somewhat awkward if tori is appreciably taller than his opponent.

Kake is performed in a manner which (allowing for the difference in arm position) is similar to tsurikomigoshi. Tori's body is tilted forward and to his left; his head is rotated toward his left shoulder; the left hand pulls strongly and continuously on uke's right lapel; and the shoulders are rotated vigorously with the chest open and the left shoulder moved well back (Fig. 22). The rotation of the shoulders casts uke strongly forward and to tori's left, dropping him to the mat.

Of course, uke's body moves in a somewhat more vertical plane

Fig. 23. ERISEOINAGE. The initial action.

than is common with koshiwaza techniques. However, it is not desirable for tori to bend his own body directly forward and seek to throw uke over the shoulder and directly to the front. Tori's body should tilt somewhat to the left, and the throw is completed with a wheeling action of the shoulders.

The shoulders alone cannot complete the throw successfully. If the back is properly arched in the initial stages and the chest well opened, the whole power of the back and loins is communicated to the throw. The action is similar to that of the schoolboy trick in which a ball of mud (uke's right shoulder) is placed on the end of a limber stick (tori's right upper arm and shoulder) and is whipped forward by the springing action of the whole length of the stick (that is, tori's back and loins).

This method of performing ipponseoinage is unquestionably the most powerful and effective. However, it makes severe demands on tori's body, particularly in the arms, chest, and lower back. Some judoka may find they are not equal to this effort, even though they may have successfully adopted the forms recommended in this study for the other rotating techniques. In such cases, it may be desirable in performing ipponseoinage to utilize the same posture, position, and manner of body movement as in the form next to be described.

Fig. 24. ERISEOINAGE. Completing the body contact.

Eriseoinage

A second form that is usually called seoinage may be distinguished by the designation of *eriseoinage,* or collar-shoulder throw. Tori's left hand grasps his opponent's sleeve, while the right grips the jacket, usually somewhat downward below the nipple rather than up near the neck. The feet advance as in ipponseoinage, if anything, moving slightly closer to uke's feet. The knees are somewhat more deeply bent, and the hips sink and move in with a sort of dip of the body— the object being to assume as low a position as practicable.

Tori's left hand pulls forward and upward on uke's right sleeve as in tsurikomigoshi. The upward action is accentuated and uke's right arm should be well raised by this pull (Fig. 23). His chest is, of course, expanded, and his left shoulder is vigorously withdrawn. As tori's body rotates in, his right hand retains its grip on the jacket, while his right elbow swings across and is inserted forcibly under uke's uplifted right arm, with the outer edge of the forearm lifted into the armpit. Tori should be careful to keep his wrist straight, and not to permit the hand to bend backward as the forearm moves into position. Although lowered at the knees, tori's trunk remains upright, and uke's body is drawn well into contact with tori's back and hip (Fig. 24).

In kake, tori straightens his knees and hoists vigorously upward

Fig. 25. ERISEOINAGE. The throw in progress.

with his hips. His body tilts to his left front (although somewhat less to the left and more nearly straight to the front than in ipponseoinage). His left hand continues to pull strongly forward and finally downward. His right shoulder and its extension, the right forearm and elbow, lift uke's right shoulder upward and forward. His head drops to his left front, following the direction of the left-hand pull (Fig. 25). His tanden remains in a powerful forward position and should not be permitted to collapse inward, driving the buttocks out and the weight back onto the heels. Uke's body will be carried forward in a circular path and will fall to the mat to tori's front. The effectiveness of this form may be increased if tori, as he moves in, strikes with the edge of his right fist and forearm against the center of uke's chest, assuming a position somewhat similar to the same stage of Tsurikomigoshi II. This impact will disturb uke's concentration and perhaps induce him to step backward while leaning his upper body forward against the impact of the forearm. In such a position, he becomes particularly vulnerable to this form. If the throw is not completed readily under the initial impetus of the attack, tori may sometimes achieve success by taking one or two very short, quick steps to the rear, thereby moving his own hips back against uke's hips and thighs and under his center of gravity. This will loosen uke's contact with the mat and increase the efficiency with which tori's hips operate as a fulcrum.

A Comparison of General Principles

It is apparent at once that ipponseoinage and eriseoinage, as they are described here, employ entirely different mechanical principles. It would appear opportune at this point to discuss these principles in general, since an understanding of the differences between them will assist the student in selecting and applying the forms which are most congenial to his individual capabilities.

This method of ipponseoinage, like the other rotating techniques described in this study, is based on the primary importance of a sudden, powerful, and continuous hand action which draws uke's body upward and forward. To facilitate such a pull, tori moves to a position somewhat farther in front of uke than is often suggested, keeping his body soft and his chest well open. In kake, tori's hips remain at or below the level they have assumed when the first body contact is made. Eriseoinage, on the other hand, requires tori to move close in and concentrate on placing himself low under his opponent's center of gravity. Kake is achieved by raising the hips under uke's body and thus levering him off the ground and into the throw.

The forms included in this study have, for the most part, been selected on the premise that the first of these two basic concepts is preferable for the majority of judoka under most circumstances. Being dependent primarily on speed and timing rather than muscular strength, they are more likely to achieve success against a physically powerful opponent. Concentration on hand action develops the ability to sense an opponent's intentions and to guide his body into a vulnerable position. Likewise, such forms facilitate the rapid exploitation of a "chance" which may arise suddenly during contest. This is often the only means of achieving a conclusive result against a strong opponent. Finally, this method usually requires *relatively* less bending of the knees and thus may be more congenial to taller men or others who have difficulty in this respect. It may be of particular value to Western judoka whose upbringing and social habits usually provide fewer opportunities for the development of strong legs than do those of the Japanese.

The hand and arm position employed in eriseoinage somewhat impairs tori's ability to exert a quick and powerful pull with the hands. Attempts to do so from this position will often impose a severe strain on tori's right arm or elbow, particularly if he is taller than his opponent. It follows that one who adopts the general principles advocated in this study will usually find it unprofitable to devote much time to practicing eriseoinage or to attempt it in contest. However, some judoka (particularly those of short stature) may not find these methods congenial and will build their whole style upon the alternate concept outlined above. In this event, they should find eriseoinage very useful.

Before leaving this subject, it is well to point out that few judoka will adopt one of these two concepts to the absolute exclusion of the other. For example, a student who learns the methods recommended in this book may nevertheless find occasion to adopt some body levering principles, either in whole (as in the third form of tsurikomigoshi previously described) or in part (as when lifting the right calf in tai-otoshi). However, it is essential to understand clearly the distinction between these two basic styles. A student who is confused in this regard may cause himself endless difficulty by seeking to combine in one throw elements which are mutually destructive.

6

Uchimata

Uchimata or "inner thigh" is an extremely powerful contest technique. However, it is difficult to bring off unless the opponent's legs are rather widely separated and is more effective if he is leaning forward at the time of the attack. It is generally more useful if employed against a relatively shorter antagonist.

In uchimata, the left hand normally holds the underside of uke's right sleeve while the right hand moves around and grips the collar at the back of the neck. As both hands pull uke forward and downward, the right foot is advanced to a position about equidistant between uke's feet and as far forward as practicable. Ideally, the toe of the right foot should be level with or even inside the toes of uke's feet. Tori's right foot should be pointed slightly to his left (Fig. 26).

From this position, tori's body commences to turn to the left and his left foot is brought to a position immediately to the rear of the right foot. The left foot rotates to the left until the toe is pointed directly toward tori's (original) rear. Tori's head turns until it is faced in this same direction, leading the body turn which presents tori's back to uke. The upper body tilts slightly forward (that is, toward the rear of tori's original position) but does not cup inward at the waist (Fig. 27).

Tori's weight transfers to his left foot as it moves into this position and the left leg is slightly bent. Tori's left arm continues to pull forward and downward. His right hand draws strongly forward on uke's collar. The effect of this action is to break uke's balance to his right front, and to draw his body forward over the position occupied by the striking leg. It is interesting to note that, in performing this movement, tori's right elbow may be raised—in contrast to all other

Fig. 26. UCHIMATA. The initial action.

FIG. 27. UCHIMATA. Moving the body and feet into position.

rotating techniques in which raising the elbow is almost always undesirable.

Simultaneously with the placing of the left foot and the transfer of weight to it, the striking action of the right leg is commenced (Fig. 28). The action of the feet appears almost as if the left foot sweeps the right foot out of the way and assumes the position formerly occupied by it. The right leg, with the toes extended and pointed downward, is raised vigorously between uke's legs, and the underside of the thigh strikes the inside of uke's left leg just at the crotch. The whole of tori's body tilts like a drawbridge, using the left hip joint as a hinge—the right hip and leg going up as the shoulders and chest go down. Tori's back remains flat and his chest must be held well open at all times. As his body tilts, tori's chin rotates sharply toward his left shoulder. A proper body turn is essential, and if tori presents only his right side to uke, he will have difficulty in succeeding with this form. His hip moves well through to uke's right, almost as if in koshiwaza proper, presenting his right buttock to uke as the latter's body is being drawn forward. The chin does not drop toward the chest; but the head remains up and the eyes look directly forward rather than down toward the ground. The right or striking leg is held as straight as possible while the left or supporting leg is bent with the knee slightly outward.

FIG. 28. UCHIMATA. The action of the leg.

Along with this movement of the legs and body the left hand continues to pull strongly downward and forward. The right hand continues to lift the collar and pulls slightly to uke's right. This combined effort tends, in effect, to rotate uke's left shoulder in a counterclockwise direction around the center of his body. As a result of this combined action, uke's left leg and the left side of his body are levered upward and in a counterclockwise direction as the right side of his body is drawn forward and downward. He is whirled through the air and dropped to the mat at what is now tori's right front corner (Fig. 29). As tori's leg swings upward in this technique, it is aimed precisely at the center between uke's legs, and strikes the inside of his left thigh only as a result of the displacement of his body caused by tori's vigorous pulling action. A strong and continuous pulling action is thus absolutely essential, both to achieve a successful throw and to protect uke from possible injury.

Uchimata II

It will be observed that this classical form of uchimata presupposes that tori will move close to and well under his opponent. However, the throw may sometimes be completed even though the opponent's strength and posture make it impossible to achieve this position. If tori finds that he is unable to place his feet as far in toward uke as he would like, he may accentuate a forward and upward pull of his right hand on uke's collar. By this means uke is drawn into close

Uchimata **65**

Fig. 29. UCHIMATA. Completing the throw.

body contact, with the front of his body against the back of tori's right hip. From this position, tori's right leg strikes the inside of uke's left leg somewhat farther down rather than high in the fork as in the usual style. Uke's left leg is not levered upward but is driven backward and outward somewhat in the manner of hanegoshi. The pull of the hands is likewise similar to a form of koshiwaza—the right elbow remaining lower so as to exert some pressure against uke's shoulder and the left hand pulling more around tori's body rather than directly downward. The only difference in result is that uke's body is not lifted so much in the air but is rotated around tori as it falls. This technique may be attempted in circumstances not usually considered apt for the employment of uchimata—that is, against an opponent whose stance is upright, whose feet are not widely separated, or who is of equal or even greater height.

Uchimata III

A useful and extremely subtle variation of uchimata may be employed when tori is moving away from uke rather than in toward him. As uke advances his right foot, tori withdraws his left. However, as uke then starts to advance his left foot, tori draws sharply forward and to his *right* with the right hand which is on uke's collar. At the same time, he does not withdraw his own right foot. As as result of this action, uke is forced to displace his left leg to his own left, leaving tori's right leg on the inside. Uke is also drawn close to tori's right side.

Just as uke's left foot reaches the ground, tori reverses the direction of his tsukuri, possibly taking advantage of uke's instinctive reaction against the original pull on his collar. He rotates his body to the left, pivots on his left foot, and drives his right leg backward, upward and outward against the inside of uke's left leg in the manner of the upright form of uchimata last described. With a similar action of his hands he rotates uke over his right thigh and drops his body to the mat.

This form is an extremely subtle one, requiring great skill and delicacy for its proper execution. If mastered, however, it is highly effective in utilizing uke's forward momentum and defeating him with a minimum of physical effort. Compared to the violent striking action of the classical uchimata, the force with which tori's leg engages that of uke is almost imperceptible.

If uchimata is not immediately successful, tori can sometimes hop forward several times on his left foot, bouncing the opponent on his uplifted thigh and maintaining or increasing the force of his hand action until the throw is achieved. This is an extremely virile method but, obviously, can be utilized only by a judoka of considerable height and exceptional physical strength.

7

Taiotoshi

Taiotoshi is one of the techniques most frequently successful in contest. It is suitable for use against a taller opponent and is effective against one whose feet are relatively close together.

Taiotoshi commences with the usual grip on collar and sleeve. The right foot is first moved across in front of the body in the same manner as in the classical form of tsurikomigoshi (Fig. 30). The left foot then moves to the rear and is placed at a point in front of and to the left of uke's left foot (Fig. 31). The precise distances will vary, of course, with tori's height and length of leg, but it is essential that this foot be placed well outside and that it not be moved back close to the line of uke's feet. If placed too close, tori will be deprived of good balance and will tend to fall forward when he attempts kake.

When the left foot arrives in position, the right is moved rapidly and firmly in a slightly circular path to a position just outside of uke's right foot (Fig. 32). It is not raised in the air but slides along the mat in a vigorous and well-controlled thrusting action. The feet assume a position in which a line between them lies at an angle of about thirty degrees from the line of uke's feet. Care must be taken that the right foot be placed just at uke's right foot rather than far past it. If this is not done, contact will be made between tori's upper leg and that of uke. This has the effect of restoring uke's broken balance and making the completion of the throw difficult. The proper point of contact between the two bodies is at the right ankles only.

There are two methods of posing the feet in taiotoshi, each of which will indicate certain changes in the other aspects of the throw.

In the first method, tori's left foot, which remains flat, is pointed directly forward or even with the toes turned slightly inward. The

Fig. 30. TAIOTOSHI. The initial action.

Fig. 31. TAIOTOSHI. Placing the left foot.

right foot also points forward with the weight on the big toe (Fig. 33). This position provides a well-balanced and solid foundation upon which a vigorous body and hand action may be based. Speaking generally, it requires that tori's feet be at somewhat more of an angle from a line through uke's feet. The need for a low body position with the knees well bent is somewhat less acute. Finally, the whole action has more of a feeling of outward drive (analogous to osotogari) and less of a feeling of rotation (which would be more analogous to the hip techniques). Taller judoka will usually find this method more congenial.

In the second method, the left foot is pivoted outward, pointed toward the left. The right foot is poised on the toes with the heel up, the knee down, and the lower leg extended along the same line as the foot and almost parallel to the ground (Fig. 34). This position will facilitate a free and vigorous turning action of the body. The left foot is usually farther back toward uke and forms a less pronounced angle with a line through uke's feet. A low position of the body and ample bending of the knees is vital, and the whole throw displays a pronounced rotary action. This form is particularly suited to shorter judoka.

Either method will succeed if well performed and selection between them is a matter of individual preference, usually dictated by the individual's stature and physical attributes. Many judoka will adopt a

Fig. 32. TAIOTOSHI. The start of the throw.   Fig. 33. TAIOTOSHI. A suggested foot position.

middle ground somewhere between the two extremes which have been described. However, it must be remembered that taiotoshi is properly a hand technique in which uke's body is cast outward, rather than a hip technique in which he is turned over tori's hip in a rotary path. The rotary method tends to bring the two bodies into contact rather than merely the ankles. This may make it easier for uke to defend by vigorously advancing his tanden and left hip. It would seem that the first method is more consistent with the rationale of taiotoshi for those whose physical conformation permits its use.

As tori rotates to conform to the movements of the feet, the hips must be lowered and the knees well bent, while the body remains upright (Fig. 32). A *relatively* low position is essential if the hand action hereinafter described is to be effective. Care must be taken that the body remains well balanced on the legs which must retain maximum flexibility, like coiled springs. For proper balance the left foreleg should remain upright with the weight on the ball of the foot. If the left knee lies forward over the foot, or if the weight falls back on the heel and tends to straighten the leg at the knee, it will indicate that the body is not in proper balance. Although the body is held upright and the tanden forward, it is helpful to drop the chin somewhat as the right foot is advanced. This adds speed to the attack, facilitates the placement of the weight on the right foot, and makes it more difficult for uke to counter by drawing

Taiotoshi   71

Fig. 34. TAIOTOSHI. Another method of placing the feet.

tori back on his heels and dropping him to the mat on his back.

It may be remarked that, after first advancing his right foot, an adept judoka can move both feet into the final position by a single jumping action, or may even eliminate the initial advance of the right foot and leap directly into the final position. However, such actions should only be attempted by one who has developed a high degree of proficiency in the orthodox technique.

It is likewise possible to pivot on the left foot without withdrawing it and to insert the right foot behind uke's right ankle in a single movement. Tori remains somewhat more upright, accentuates the leading action of his hips, and drives uke almost directly to the side rather than toward the latter's right front. This form is closely analogous to osotogari and is often particularly suitable for taller judoka who possess powerful hands. Care must be taken not to place the right foot too far past uke's ankle. If this is done, the throw becomes neither taiotoshi nor osotogari, but an undesirable mixture of the two which can only be accomplished by exerting vastly superior strength.

Tsukuri is commenced simultaneously with the initial movement of the right foot. The first action is a pull forward and upward with both hands. Tori's arms are moved upward and outward with the elbows lifted to the side and the chest well opened. As tori's body turn continues, the right arm drops quickly, placing the forearm low against uke's chest, from which position the right hand asserts a constant pressure upward against uke's jaw (Fig. 31). This forces uke upward and to his right, much in the manner of osotogari.

This upward and outward drive must be carefully distinguished from the right-hand action in hip techniques. In koshiwaza, the right arm will bend at the elbow, drawing uke forward over a vertical forearm. In taiotoshi (after the preliminary pull described above) the right arm drives upward and outward, tending to straighten at the elbow,

Fig. 35. TAIOTOSHI. The throw in progress.

and move in an arc over and around tori's right foot (Fig. 35). Care must be taken to move uke's body around this point, and not to press his left shoulder directly to his rear.

Tori's left hand draws uke's right arm outward and slightly downward in a circular path (Fig. 35). The effect of this action is to break uke's balance to his right front and impart a whirling motion to his body which tends to pivot it around the single contact made by the right ankles. The action by the left hand is also distinct from that common with hip techniques. It is a serious fault if this hand draws uke's right arm inward around tori's body. When this is done, tori will invariably bend forward at the waist while his thighs and buttocks remain close to uke. The latter can thus defend successfully by advancing his own waist and remaining in an upright position. Some judoka find it useful in avoiding this fault to think of the left hand at the start of the attack as if it were attempting to draw uke almost directly toward the latter's right. Then, as tori turns his body, the left hand will automatically fall into the proper circular path around the point where the feet are in contact, and uke will be drawn into the throw with little opportunity to assert his strength in defense. This use of the left hand is difficult to learn, since it requires the exertion of considerable strength in a somewhat unusual direction. However, its mastery is essential to the achievement of good form with taiotoshi.

Kake is performed by a vigorous continuance of this rotary motion of the hands and body. To obtain sufficient power, the hand action must be supported by:

1. The backward rotation of tori's left shoulder, which accentuates the open chest position; and

2. A strong and continuous rotary motion of the hips. It is helpful to conceive of tori's right hip as the source of power for the right hand, transmitted along a straight line running from this hip, through the right forearm, to the side of uke's jaw. It is obvious that such a vigorous action can be achieved only if the whole body is upright and well balanced on the feet. The right hand can be effective only if the knees are well bent, permitting its action to be primarily upward rather than horizontal.

This hand, hip, and shoulder action is, of course, limited to the needs of a tewaza technique—that is, primarily as a source of a powerful outward driving force. It should not be carried to such a degree that uke's body will be drawn in against tori's and wound around it, even by those who stress the rotary aspects of the throw.

As the whirling action of the technique unfolds, tori's head drops even further toward his chest directly to the front, and his right shoulder is lifted, adding power to the action of the right hand. It will be observed that the head does not rotate as far to tori's left shoulder as is customary in most techniques involving body rotation, but acts in a manner somewhat similar to sode-tsurikomigoshi, in which uke's body is cast outward rather than being rotated around the hip. If the throw is correctly performed, uke's body will seem to hesitate for a moment and then be whirled with great speed over tori's right ankle. The effectiveness of this form can be enhanced if, at the moment of kake, tori imparts a slight spring to his right calf, thereby assisting in the removal of the support which uke derives from his right foot. This can be accomplished most readily by forcing the right heel down to the mat, thereby straightening the leg at the knee and raising the calf against uke's ankle. This action is relatively slight and if exaggerated, might seriously impair the effort by inducing tori to straighten his right leg too much, thereby raising his right hip. Therefore it may be well not to attempt this refinement until the more important aspects of the throw have been thoroughly learned.

A few judoka may find it useful to adopt an entirely different sort of hand action for use in connection with this leg movement. Tori advances in the usual way, but remains as low as possible with his knees well bent, and emphasizes the spring of his right calf. Simultaneously with this leg movement, tori's right hand drives straight upward, and his left hand pulls directly downward in the direction of his right thigh. This produces a violent and close-coupled throw, turning uke's body sharply in the air and dropping it close in front of tori.

Despite its effectiveness, this form is of limited utility because it can be successfully employed only by the relatively shorter judoka with exceptional strength and leg flexibility. If this form is attempted by one without a physique to which it is congenial, uke's right arm will invariably be drawn in against tori's body while tori will collapse his own waist inward and project his buttocks outward. This reduces tori's ability to exert power and makes an effective defense much more probable.

A common defect in taiotoshi is the failure of tori's body to move far enough to uke's left in the early stages of the throw. This defect will have two unfortunate consequences. First, tori's right foot will tend to be placed too far outside uke's right foot, producing a contact of the upper leg or body and blocking the throw. Second, tori's right hip and side will fall into place ahead of his right elbow, thereby eliminating much of the power which must be exerted against uke's jaw by the right hand and arm. The following is an effective solution to this difficulty.

Instead of advancing the right foot across in front of his body as usual at the commencement of the technique, tori places it farther to his right, just inside the extension of uke's left foot. The toes are pointed to tori's left in a position somewhat similar to that assumed in the initial stages of osotogake. As tori now executes the throw in the usual manner, his body will automatically be fixed in a position farther to uke's left than usual. Although careful practice is necessary if tori is to avoid running into uke's right foot as he slides his own right foot into place, most judoka will find this method more effective than the usual style.

In seeking to attain the same objective, (i.e., placing the body more to uke's left) some judoka will eliminate the initial movement of the right foot entirely. The action will be commenced by withdrawing the left foot in the usual circular path. The right foot merely pivots to conform to the turn of tori's body and then is slid into position in the usual way. This form is particularly effective if uke has advanced his own right foot vigorously and displaced his own weight well forward over it. By eliminating one movement, it may also increase the speed with which the throw can be given effect.

Taiotoshi **75**

In passing, it might be pointed out that this sort of foot action *(i.e.,* the initial withdrawing of the left foot in a circular path) may sometimes be employed in the hip techniques, notably tsurikomigoshi. Some judoka will find that they can move into their throws more rapidly and easily in this way. The danger is, of course, that, in rotating away from uke's right side, tori will fail to get his hip far enough through to provide the necessary fulcrum. This is not a serious matter in taiotoshi where the contact is at the ankle, but may be fatal to success with tsurikomigoshi or other forms where the hip placement is critical. It should only be attempted by judoka who have learned to maintain maximum continuous control of their opponent's body by a powerful hand action.

Taiotoshi may be effectively performed with tori's right elbow inserted under uke's right armpit *(i.e.,* seoiotoshi) or by inserting the whole arm *(i.e.,* ipponseoiotoshi), and some judoka find these methods particularly suitable to their physical makeup. Those who adopt these methods (and particularly the latter) must exercise extreme care to keep the body upright, the tanden forward, and the chest expanded because the tendency to drag the opponent to the ground instead of making a clean throw is always present when these arm positions are carelessly used.

8

Osotogari

In osotogari the left hand grasps the sleeve on the outside and just below the elbow. The right hand takes a full grip on the jacket just above uke's left nipple. The wrist of the right hand is cocked down with the hand tilted up.

Tori advances his left foot and places it with the toes approximately three inches in front of and twelve inches to the outside of the toes of uke's right foot. It is not to be lifted from the mat but slides smoothly into position with the foot flat and the knee bent. The foot does not toe in or out, but remains parallel with the line of the leg. However, foot and leg move in an outward direction toward uke's right rear at an angle of about thirty degrees rather than straight to his rear (Fig. 36). A taller judoka may place his foot somewhat farther to the front or outside of uke's right foot, but care should be taken never to advance it past uke's right foot or to move too close beside it. This recommended technique is distinct in this respect from that frequently taught in which tori attacks straight toward uke's rear, more in the manner of osoto-otoshi.

As the foot is advanced, tori's body moves forward in the same direction with the head erect, the back upright, the tanden forward, the chest open, the hips rotated slightly toward the left, and the body and hips slightly lowered as a result of the bent left knee. The leading and forward position of the tanden is of great importance and any tendency to collapse inward at the waist when the right leg swings forward will be fatal to success. A helpful concept is to conceive of the hips as being opened or separated as the center of the tanden advances.

It is likewise vital that the head remain upright and back of a line drawn vertically through the opponent's right hip. If this is not done,

Fig. 36. OSOTOGARI. The initial tsukuri.   Fig. 37. OSOTOGARI. The action of the right hand.

it will develop two weaknesses in the attack—the body will bend inward at the waist and make a powerful sweep difficult; and the body will move ahead of the right hand, sometimes extending the right arm with elbow straight across uke's chest rather than permitting the hand and arm to concentrate its push against the left side of uke's chin and chest. It is often valuable to accentuate this head position in practice, even to the point of directing the eyes upward during uchikomi, but this exaggeration cannot be safely indulged in in contest, since it renders tori susceptible to a counterthrow.

Simultaneously with these movements, tori's right hand makes a slight movement, drawing the jacket slightly outward and forward. It completes the fishhook and moves strongly inward and upward against uke's throat and the lower left side of his jaw. The arm is not straightened but is allowed to bend so that the length of the forearm is pressed against the left front corner of uke's chest below his left armpit (Fig. 37). Tori's right elbow should be neither raised to the outside nor placed against the middle or front of uke's chest.

The primary immediate objective of this right-hand action is to rotate uke's chin toward his right shoulder and tilt his head to the right. In turn, this will break uke's balance in the proper direction (that is, to his right rear) and will hold him in position with his weight on the right foot until it can be swept away. In practice, tori should concentrate his attention on achieving this displacement of the head.

Fig. 38. OSOTOGARI. Advancing the right leg.

The right-hand action may be ineffective if it utilizes only the strength of the hand and arm. It will be recalled that the body is lowered as the left foot advances. This enables tori to concentrate the strength of his whole right side behind the hand and elbow. Thus he utilizes the expansive force of the body in disturbing uke's balance. Care must be taken that this expansion develops from the bent knees and that the left foot remains flat rather than rising on the toes.

Concurrently with this right-hand action, tori's left hand pulls uke's right arm in toward tori's body and either downward toward the waist or sideward across tori's body, depending on individual preference. This action of the left hand must be felt all the way up to the shoulder and must accentuate the opening of the chest. This expanding chest position is of great importance in that it tends to mobilize the full power of the shoulder and chest muscles behind the right hand.

If tori elects to pull downward with the left hand, in the more accepted style, he may find that the ability to exert a strong continuous pressure is reduced as the left hand moves lower and the wrist is compelled to curl. To achieve a stronger result, the heel of the left hand may rotate inward as the hand moves downward. The wrist is thus cocked instead of curling and the arm is straightened at the elbow. This places the strength of the whole arm and shoulder against uke's right sleeve, making it extremely difficult for him to withdraw his weight from his right foot and restore his balance.

Osotogari   79

The effect of the combined action of both hands and body is to disturb uke's balance to his right rear and somewhat upward. If properly executed, uke's weight will be fixed on the outside of his right heel. It is particularly important to note that the direction of tori's attack should be at an angle toward uke's right rear rather than directly to the rear. While the latter method is employed by many of the older masters and described in most orthodox textbooks, it is less effective in that more physical strength is required and tori is more open to a counter.

As uke's balance is broken, tori threads his right hip through the opening at the right side of uke's body and projects his right foot to uke's right rear (Fig. 38). The tanden and rotating hips lead this movement with the hip remaining low and the right foot swings forward near the ground with the toe pointed and without excessive bending or lifting of the right knee. As tori's foot moves forward, the toes are turned slightly to the left, thereby assisting the hips in the slight leftward rotation described above. Tori retains constant tsukuri with both hands, thereby drawing the two bodies into chest and hip contact and preventing uke from regaining his balance. However, tori's right arm remains bent and does not uncoil against uke's head.

At this point, tori is ready to perform kake. With his right leg extended to uke's right rear, and with the toes pointed slightly to the left, he sweeps the leg strongly to his rear in a slightly circular movement, aided by a rotating action of the hips to the right (Fig. 39). During the sweep, the leg should be slightly bent at the knee to lend flexibility to its action, but should not be hooked at the knee. The toes should remain pointed throughout the sweep and it is somewhat helpful to feel the top of the foot, with the toes extended and somewhat curled, drive *downward* against the back of uke's calf.

Tori's leg makes contact just at the bottom of uke's right calf. Tori's foot does not touch the ground but continues in a backward and upward direction. Simultaneously tori, by lifting his right shoulder and extending his right arm, drives powerfully against uke's throat and jaw, forcing the latter's head and upper body still further toward his right rear. Concurrently with the leg sweep, tori's head drops sharply to his chest and slightly to his left. The whole of tori's upper body moves forward and downward in a sharp explosion of power, balanced on tori's firmly planted left foot, and drives uke to the mat.

Fig. 39. OSOTOGARI. The throw.

The sweep of the leg is not merely a matter of brute force but, with long practice, can become an extremely subtle effort. Timing is of vital importance. If the leg contact comes too soon (that is, before uke has been brought to a state of maximum instability) a strong opponent may retain enough balance to take control of tori's leg with his own, reverse the direction of the movement, and throw tori with an extremely hard counter. If the contact comes too late, uke may have an opportunity to recover his balance, escape by tai-sabaki—a turning of the body, and place himself in a position to counter.

The leg contact itself is not a blow, as with a heavy swinging weapon, but is more in the nature of a plucking—comparable to the manner in which an expert with a stockwhip might remove a cork from a bottle. A master can refine this form to such a point that he tightens his own calf just at the instant of contact and seems almost to grip uke's leg with these calf muscles and snatch it swiftly from the ground.

Depending on speed rather than sheer muscle, this method materially reduces the violence of the contact between the two bodies, but still will produce a sudden and severe throw. The same concept may be employed in all waza where tori's foot or lower leg engages the lower leg of uke and is helpful to some degree even where the contatc is made at the back of the knees.

It is interesting to note that many authorities recommend that the contact be made at the thigh rather than the calf. It would seem, however, that such a method, which relies on power of leg rather than effective breaking of uke's balance before the sweep is attempted, is less in accord with the basic principle of judo—that is, to achive maximum effect with a minimum of muscular effort.

Two faults frequently observed in osotogari are:

(1) Tori places his advanced right foot on the ground behind uke and seeks to push him over it; and

(2) Tori permits a considerable distance to open between his body and that of uke, and then seeks to drag him down by tugging with the arms.

Both faults arise from the same basic error—a failure to take immediate control of uke's body with the hands and then to bring it to a state of maximum instability before performing kake.

The effectiveness of osotogari may sometimes be greatly enhanced by an adjustment in the relative positions of the two contestants at the beginning of the throw. It has been pointed out that a successful osotogari depends upon the forcible application of tori's right hand against the left side of uke's neck and jaw. If the two contestants are directly opposite each other when the throw commences, there is a tendency for tori's body to move forward past his right hand. If this occurs, the force of the body is removed from behind the right-hand action, causing the elbow to drop back or lift, and placing the whole muscular strain of this effort on the arm and particularly the junction of the arm with the shoulder. It is extremely difficult to break the balance of even a moderately strong opponent in this way.

However if tori, immediately before commencing osotogari, manages to move his body slightly to the right, outside the line of uke's body, the weight of tori's body is placed *behind* the right elbow rather than beside it. As he then advances the left foot, the whole force of his body is directed from his right hip, through the right elbow, up along the forearm, and is applied directly against uke's jaw. In this way it is much easier to break the balance of even a powerful opponent and to continue the pressure against him until the leg sweep can be made. In order not to forewarn the opponent, this move must be made in a subtle and almost imperceptible manner. However, even a slight displacement to the right will have a substantial effect on the success of the throw.

Fig. 40. OSOTOGAKE. Moving into position.

Osotogake

A more specific application of this principle is found in the variation commonly known as osotogake. In this form, the right foot is first moved to the right and slightly forward, with the toes pointed somewhat to the left. Tori may sometimes prepare for this attack by permitting the right foot to move somewhat to the right of its normal position in the course of a natural advancing or retreating step. The left foot is then rotated backward to a position behind and just to the left of the right heel, with the toes pointed to the left almost parallel with the original line of tori's feet (Fig. 40). The position of the feet is similar to that assumed in the early stages of kouchigari. Tori's body is moved to his opponent's left in front of or even outside uke's left foot. It is rotated so that tori faces to uke's right and directly across in front of the latter's body. Simultaneously with this movement, the left hand pulls uke's right arm strongly downward and inward while the right hand pushes upward against uke's right lower jaw. The inward turn of the left wrist and straightening of the left arm previously described is of particular value in this technique. The effect of this hand action is to cause uke's body to bend to the right, with his right waist bowed slightly inward. His weight is thus firmly fixed on his right foot and the weight of his upper body is unbalanced over it.

Osotogari   83

Fig. 41. OSOTOGAKE. Advancing the right leg.

Fig. 42. OSOTOGAKE. The throw in progress with impetus principally to the side and leg contact near the knee.

From this position, without moving the left foot as in the usual osotogari, tori's right foot moves across the front of uke's body with the tanden forward, the hips rotated slightly to the left, and the toes pointed in the usual way (Fig. 41). The throw can be completed with a sweep *(gari)* striking at the calf, or with a hook *(gake)* in which tori's right knee engages at the back of uke's right knee. There is somewhat less impetus given to this leg than the full rearward sweep found in the orthodox osotogari. Tori's hooking action tends rather to scoop up uke's right leg, picking it off the ground, and locking it back of tori's bent right knee (Fig. 42). It may be helpful to consider that this leg action is similar to that employed in ouchigari while the sweeping action in the orthodox osotogari has more in common with the use of the leg in haraigoshi.

As the hooking action occurs, it may be found helpful to slide the foot down the back of uke's calf, keeping the toe pointed and the foot curled back. This brings the full force of the hooking action against the lower and weaker portion of uke's leg, and may make it easier to remove his foot from the mat.

As his right leg moves forward, tori's upper body reacts in a similar manner to that previously described. The right arm drives vigorously upward and forward against the lower right of uke's jaw, supported by the expanding action of the body and the lifting right shoulder;

the left hand continues to pull downward and inward; the hips rotate slightly to the left and reverse their rotation as the right leg hooks; and the head drops sharply to the chest as the upper body moves forward and the right leg backward. Uke is usually thrown somewhat farther to his right rear rather than falling almost at the point where he originally stood, as in the orthodox form.

The distinguishing features of the osotogake technique are: (1) To attack uke from a position somewhat to his left; (2) to break his body inward at the right hip, fixing his weight on his right foot; and (3) to attack rapidly with the hooked right leg without advancing the left foot. These principles have wide application, particularly for a relatively tall judoka. They constitute a weapon of opportunity which may often be used when the opponent is off balance as a result of his unsuccessful attack, but seems out of reach of more usual forms. It is also an excellent form of second-intention attack and can be quickly adopted after an abortive attempt at tsurikomigoshi.

The initial movements of the feet which have been described (i.e., advancing the right foot and withdrawing the left) are mechanically correct and are highly useful in studying the technique. However, it should be pointed out that this somewhat exaggerated form is neither absolutely necessary nor even always desirable in contest. Experienced judoka may find it more effective merely to pivot on the ball of the left foot without changing its position on the mat, rotate the hips slightly to the left, and move directly into the attack with the tanden well forward.

Osotogari II

Another effective variation of osotogari is particularly suitable for taller judoka who find the orthodox form somewhat confining.

In this technique tori grasps uke's jacket with both hands, taking a full grip of the cloth just below the shoulders and in front of the armpits rather than on the collar itself. The left foot is advanced in the usual way, but should be placed somewhat farther to uke's front, in order that there may be ample space to execute the drawing action required by this form.

As tori's foot advances, he draws uke forward, upward and to uke's right. This action must be sudden and extremely vigorous. While taking care not to rise on the left toes nor to straighten the left knee, tori's body expands upward and his chest is well opened. Both elbows

Fig. 43. OSOTOGARI II. The preparatory action of an alternate method.

will be raised outward in executing the pull. This is particularly apparent in the left arm which pulls strongly across in front of tori's expanded chest (Fig. 43). The action of tori's right hand must start in a slightly outward circular path, drawing uke forward and to his *left* for just an instant before breaking his balance in the opposite direction. If tori's chest is properly expanded, this brings into play the muscles of his shoulders and back, in addition to the wrist and arm.

The effect of this action is twofold. First, uke's balance is broken more to his right side than to the right rear as in the orthodox form, and his weight is moved onto the outside of his right foot rather than backward on to the heel. Second, a firm body contact is achieved between the right side of tori's chest (which has been kept well open by the pull of the arms) and the right front side of uke's chest. It will be observed that, since uke's body has been tilted to the side and raised upward, an aperture still will remain between the two bodies from the hips downward.

While holding uke's body in this unbalanced position and in close contact with his own, tori threads his right leg through this aperture and performs the leg sweep. By reason of the different positions of the two bodies, the leg contact will probably not be made at the calf, as in the orthodox form, but will extend up the leg to the thigh. Also, tori's body and hips will turn somewhat to his left during the sweep, thereby giving the whole action a feeling somewhat like that of harai-

86　Mechanics of Judo

Fig. 44. SODE-OSOTOGARI. The action of the left hand.

goshi. The key to success with this form is to maintain the tsukuri until the leg sweep is performed. Uke's body must be held up, and in an off-balanced position. If tori fails to maintain a continuous pull with his hands, uke can move his weight back off the toes to a well-balanced position and successfully resist the attack. As the leg sweep is commenced, tori's right hand drives strongly against the side of the jaw, turning and tilting the head toward uke's right shoulder. The left hand moves downward and toward uke's right rear, thus achieving both a powerful pull by its grip on the jacket and some pressure with the back of the hand and forearm against the front of uke's shoulder. This hand action completes the destruction of uke's balance and accomplishes the throw.

Sode-osotogari

The following modification might well be designated as sode-oso-togari. It is often extremely useful for judoka who wish to attack uke's *left* leg without reversing the normal hand position. In this form the right hand remains on the collar as usual. However, the left hand is shifted to the underside of uke's right sleeve, or may seize the inside of the sleeve in the same manner as has been previously described for sode-tsurikomigoshi. Tori commences the form by advancing his right foot in the usual way required for an attack to this side. However, with the initial movement of foot and body, tori's left hand lifts strongly upward, raising his opponent's right arm high in the air (Fig. 44).

Osotogari 87

Fig. 45. SODE-OSOTOGARI. The throw in progress, seen from Uke's rear.

His forearm is placed along the underside of the arm with his elbow at or near the armpit, just as in sode-tsurikomigoshi. His right hand draws the left lapel downward and toward his own advancing waist, in the same general direction as is indicated for the left (or sleeve-gripping) hand in the usual osotogari attack previously described. As his body advances, tori's left hand continues to lift and move to his right; its object being to carry uke's right elbow across over the top of the latter's head (Fig. 45). The movement can be visualized by considering uke's right arm as the spoke of a large wheel which tori seeks to revolve in a clockwise direction.

The effect of this hand action is to unbalance uke's whole upper body to his left and fix his weight far over on his left foot. From this position, tori can readily complete the osotogari in the usual fashion.

Of course, raising the right arm of a really strong opponent in this fashion is not easy. Tori must be alert to discover in uke's movements an opportunity for this action, and can take advantage of it only by a particularly smooth and rapid action. However, the form has numerous advantages. Since it moves against uke's left side from a hand position, which normally indicates an attack in the opposite direction, it has substantial surprise value, and adds to the versatility of tori's attack. Likewise, judoka who are accustomed to move only to

the right may find the relatively free movements of this throw somewhat easier on the body than an attempt at a more orthodox form
in this unfamiliar direction.

This type of hand action need not be confined to osotogari, but may
be found useful in almost any type of attack against the outside of uke's
left leg, such as osotogake, haraigoshi, taiotoshi, or even tsurikomiashi.

9

Kosotogari

Kosotogari in its common form is well known and frequently described in the textbooks. In brief, tori first advances his left foot to a position outside of uke's right and moves his own right foot behind it to approximately the position formerly occupied by the left, turning his body in a half-circle to his right, so that it faces the right front corner of uke's body. He pulls downward on uke's right sleeve and pushes upward and forward against uke's chest and chin with his own right hand, thus breaking uke's balance to his right rear and fixing his weight on his right foot. From this position, tori sweeps uke's right foot forward with the sole of his own left, while the hand action drives uke to the ground to the right rear. In a variation, better described as kosotogake, tori moves somewhat less to uke's right side, and hooks the back of uke's right knee with his own left rather than sweeping it.

While it may of course be successful on occasions, this form contains intrinsic mechanical weaknesses. The platform leg *(i.e.,* the right) being on the inside interferes with the free sweep of the striking leg, and the movement of tori's body to the side makes it difficult for him to exert a powerful action with the right hand. Sometimes one can obtain more power by reversing the grip of the hands and using the right hand (as in sodetsurikomigoshi) to raise uke's left arm high from a grip on the sleeve as the throw is done. This is somewhat more powerful if it can be achieved, but it is difficult to raise the arm of the opponent in this way and only a relatively short and extremely strong judoka can have much hope of doing so.

Thus, it will be seen that some radical improvement of the orthodox form is necessary if the benefits of an attack from the kosotogari posi-

Fig. 46. KOSOTOGARI I. The initial position.

tion are to be attained. One method of doing so is the following unusual form.

Kosotogari I

In attacking in the same direction, that is, against uke's right leg, the normal grip on his jacket is reversed. Tori's left hand grips high on uke's right collar or around toward the back of his neck in a manner similar to that employed in uchimata. His right hand takes a full grip of the cloth on the outside of uke's left sleeve. The hand is not on the underside of the sleeve with the thumb out in the usual style, but grips with the line of the knuckles upright (as in shaking hands) and the thumb on the inside against uke's arm (Fig. 46).

Tori first advances his left foot to a position past uke's right foot and, if possible, moves it inward so that it lies behind uke's right heel. Obviously the technique will be difficult to perform unless uke's right foot is somewhat advanced. Tori's right foot is then advanced in a slightly rotary direction and placed with its instep behind his left heel. The toes of the right foot are pointed to tori's right, approximately parallel to a line drawn through uke's feet. Both knees bend in order that tori's body may be lowered.

As the foot movement takes place, tori's hips and tanden are moved forward against uke's body. The hips are lowered so that the tanden makes contact with uke's abdomen below the latter's center of gravity. As tori's right foot moves into position, his weight will move back

Fig. 47. KOSOTOGARI I. Ready for the throw.

upon it to free the left foot for a sweep and furnish a firm platform for lifting action. Care must be taken, however, that the position of tori's body is not altered by this transfer of weight since, if it is allowed to rock back, the necessary body contact will be lost. The only change is a relative one of balance between the feet.

Simultaneously with this action of feet and body, tori's left hand pulls strongly downward on uke's collar, while his right hand forces uke's left arm backward and inward, seeking to follow a clockwise circular path around the center of uke's body. The effect of this hand action is to break uke's balance toward his right rear corner, bend his body inward at the waist on his right side, and fix him in close body contact with tori's tanden.

From this position, kake is performed in a violent outburst of power. Tori's left leg engages the back of its knee at the back of uke's right knee and hooks it strongly forward. Simultaneously tori drives inward and upward with his right hand against uke's left arm and body. Tori's right elbow is kept close to his own hip and serves as a conduit for the power of his body (Fig. 47). His body drives upward, impelled by the lifting and expanding action of his loins and knees.

As a result of this action, uke's left foot is lifted from the ground and his whole body is rendered unstable. Tori's chin drops forward and he continues to pull downward with his left hand and to press inward with his left as the hooking action is completed. Uke's right foot is swept from the ground, his body is rotated somewhat in a clockwise

Kosotogari 93

direction, and he is cast to the mat to his right rear. As in osotogari, the direction of the attack is not directly to the rear, but at an angle toward uke's right rear corner.

This technique is dependent primarily upon the lifting action of tori's body. If it is properly performed, uke will be thrown violently over tori's left knee, even though the hooking action may have exerted little force against his leg. Utilizing the power of the body and minimizing the importance of the leg sweep, it would seem to be more promising for use against a strong opponent than the usual style. Since the attack is made against the leg on the same side on which tori grasps uke's *collar*, rather than on the sleeve side as in the usual form, this style has a tactical value. A judoka who grips in the normal fashion for an attack against uke's right leg *(i.e.,* left hand on sleeve and right hand on collar) may, without warning his opponent by changing this grip, mount a powerful attack to the opposite side against uke's *left* leg. This kosotogari to uke's left as a second intention attack, after an attempt of osotogari against his right leg, can be extremely effective.

The problem with this form is that it requires tori to move low under uke's center of gravity and exert a powerful upward thrusting action. A tall man will probably find this difficult, and thus the form is usually most effective for judoka who are relatively shorter than their opponents. One who usually finds himself against those of shorter stature should find the following method more valuable.

Kosotogari II

Tori grips uke's jacket with both hands at the lapels, preferably with his left hand over uke's right, and his right hand inside uke's left arm. To perform tsukuri, his left hand pulls downward and his left elbow presses in. This locks uke's right arm in place, forces his right waist inward, and draws his right shoulder outward past his hip. The right hand and forearm drives upward against uke's chest and chin. The hand action is similar to that used in osotogari and is designed to achieve the same result, that is, to break uke's balance to his right rear and to bend his body somewhat inward at his waist on the right. It is important that the whole of the right forearm, all the way to the elbow, is driven against uke's chest (Fig. 48).

As the hand action commences, tori moves his left foot and leg forward to the outside of uke's right, the action being much the same

Fig. 48. KOSOTOGARI II. The initial position.

Fig. 49. KOSOTOGARI II. The throw.

as in osotogari (except, of course, that the outer rather than the inner leg is advanced). His tanden is well forward, and his stomach and right hip come in strong contact with uke's tanden, right hip, and right upper thigh. The body action is again very similar to osotogari except that (since the inner leg does not have to pass between the two bodies) the waists and hips of the contestants meet.

In performing kake, tori's right hand and forearm drive violently against uke, forcing the right side of his body upward. The left hand continues to draw uke's right lapel downward. Tori's left leg sweeps backward engaging uke's right leg at about the top of the calf. Tori's tanden projects itself violently forward and downward, as if to push uke's middle down to the ground. The countering action of tori's hands and body (both of which now force uke's upper body downward and to the rear) while his leg draws uke's in the opposite direction, seems to pivot uke's body around a point somewhere in the vicinity of his upper thigh and drops him forcibly to the mat (Fig. 49).

A unique feature of this form is the manner in which tori seems to grasp his opponent's body between his left leg applied to the back of uke's calf and his tanden applied to the front of uke's body at the waist. The shearing action of these two contacts moving in opposite directions supplies a substantial part of the impetus for the throw. Although it would of course be impossible to do so in randori or contest, an expert can demonstrate the principle of this form effectively by attacking and throwing with the use of the leg and body alone.

The throw requires an all-out commitment to the attack by tori, who often goes to the ground with his opponent. It has considerable tactical advantage in that it enables an adept, who grips with both hands on the jacket, to attack in either osotogari or kosotogari on both sides without warning his opponent by a change of hand position.

10

Ouchigari

Ouchigari or major internal reaping is commenced from the usual position with the right hand at the lapel and the left hand on the sleeve.

Ouchigari I

Tori's right foot is first moved forward to a position inside of and parallel with uke's left foot. The movement is made with the tanden leading, the body upright and the knees slightly bent. The foot should be two or three inches from uke's left foot and as deep as possible, preferably with the toes level with uke's heel. Tori's left foot is then placed directly behind his right, with the toes pointed to the left, the instep opposite the right heel and the foot flat (Fig. 50). Care must be taken to advance this foot well forward, within two or three inches of the right heel if possible. The left knee remains slightly bent and the weight is permitted to shift onto this foot when it reaches the proper position, thereby freeing the right leg for the attack. Care must be taken at this point that the shift of weight does not affect the position of the body. The forward aspect of the body, and particularly of the tanden, must not be altered.

With the initial movement of the right foot, the right hand draws uke slightly upward and to his left. The elbow is allowed to bend as tori moves in, and the forearm is placed against uke's chest. Its proper position is somewhat to the center of the chest, so as to permit uke to be forced to his left rear. Tori's left hand draws uke's right arm downward and inward in the direction of his (tori's) own advancing left hip. The bending of the knees and the leading action of the tanden

Fig. 50. OUCHIGARI I. Advancing into position.

Fig. 51. OUCHIGARI I. The throw in progress.

give tori the feeling of being somewhat under his opponent and of driving somewhat upward as well as to the left rear.

Kake is performed by raising the right foot from the mat and hooking the right knee at the back of uke's left knee. The right leg then drives backward, lifting uke's left leg from the mat (Fig. 51). Tori's right leg remains bent, locking uke's left in the angle at the back of tori's knee. As tori drives forward, his right knee drops slightly toward the mat. It may be noted that, if tori is much taller than his opponent, he may find this interlocking at the knees difficult. Under such circumstances, it may be more satisfactory to attack with the back of tori's ankle against uke's lower leg, even though this method is generally less effective than that described above.

As the reaping action of the leg is made, tori's whole body drives forward against uke, forcing the latter to his left rear. The right hand and forearm press strongly against uke's chest while the left hand (relatively less important in this form) retains its tension on uke's right arm in order to keep the two bodies in close contact. Tori's chin drops forward in the direction of uke's left shoulder, leading his whole body in a violent movement which throws uke to the mat.

If tori permits uke's body to move out of contact with his own, or if he drives forward to the full extension of his left leg before completing the throw, a successful result cannot be achieved. Tori may sometimes correct this defect and maintain the impetus of his attack by

98   Mechanics of Judo

Fig. 52. OUCHIGARI II. Preparing for an alternate method.

Fig. 53. OUCHIGARI II. The throw toward uke's right rear.

hopping forward on his left foot as he completes the required action of leg, hands, and body.

Ouchigari II

While the action described above is the accepted classical form of ouchigari, some judoka find the following variation useful. The action of the feet and body is identical up to the commencement of kake but a different hand movement is employed. The right hand and forearm drive against uke's chest as before but in an inward direction (to uke's *right* rear) rather than outward (Fig. 52). The forearm must thus be placed, not at the center of uke's chest, but on its left side, with the hand below the jaw much in the manner of osotogari. The effect is thus to shift uke's balance to his right rear and onto his right foot rather than to his left. In kake, tori's head will drop toward uke's right shoulder rather than his left, leading tori's body in the same direction; the right hand and arm also drive toward uke's right rear corner; and the hooking action of the leg is utilized to tilt uke's body toward, the opposite corner (Fig. 53). Uke is thus thrown to his right rather than to his left. The difference in the two forms is exemplified by the different functions of the reaping leg. In the classical form, this leg acts to remove a support from under uke's body and drop him where the support has been. In the modified form, the

Ouchigari **99**

Fig. 54. OUCHIGARI III. Tori prepares to attack while moving to the rear.

Fig. 55. OUCHIGARI III. The leg and body in position.

reaping action uses uke's left leg as a lever to tilt his body over the right leg which has been fixed in place by the tsukuri and is not itself attacked at all. Although generally less satisfactory than the classical style, this technique may be more suitable to certain physical types. A judoka who is consistently taller than his opponents, and therefore finds it somewhat more difficult to place his weight under theirs, may find this method easier to apply successfully. Even if unsuccessful, a strong attempt at this form often opens the way for an effective second-intention attack with taiotoshi.

Ouchigari III

A third and entirely distinct form of ouchigari is employed by tori when moving backward rather than forward. As the two contestants move together, tori's left leg retreats as uke's right leg advances (Fig. 54). As uke is about to advance his left leg, tori does not withdraw his right, but pulls uke forward and downward with both hands, the right hand drawing uke to his left and fixing his weight on his left or advanced foot. Simultaneously, tori advances his right foot and hooks the right knee behind uke's left knee, in the same manner that would be employed in an orthodox ouchigari (Fig. 55). Tori then reaps uke's leg strongly forward and *inward* (that is, toward tori's left); pulls strongly downward on uke's left lapel; and with his left hand forces uke's right arm backward and inward in a circular path. This combination of forces causes uke's body to rotate in a clockwise direction *(i.e.,* with his left side going forward and downward while his right side is forced backward and toward his left). Uke's body will be whirled around and thrown to the mat, usually in a position almost at right angles to his original line of movement.

It is possible that uke will be surprised by this sort of attack since it is performed while he is moving forward and tori backward, rather than the reverse which is common with ouchigari. While by no means as powerful as the more usual methods, it is a subtle and effective technique and makes the maximum use of uke's own forward motion to upset him.

11

Kouchigari

Kouchigari, or minor internal reaping, should be attempted only against an opponent whose legs are rather widely separated and preferably when the leg to be attacked is somewhat advanced. The classical form of kouchigari is performed as follows:

Kouchigari I

With the hands in the usual grip on the opponent's right sleeve and left lapel, the left hand pulls strongly downward on uke's right sleeve. The right hand pulls downward and at the same time presses uke to the rear and slightly to his right (Fig. 56). The object of this action is to fix all of uke's weight on his right foot. To facilitate this action, tori's right shoulder is slightly lowered as his body turns in against his opponent, and both knees should be slightly bent.

Simultaneously with the commencement of the hand action, the right foot is advanced to a position between the opponent's feet. It should be placed well forward with the toes past the toes of uke's right foot; slightly closer to uke's right foot than his left; and with the toes pointed slightly to the left.

The left foot is then rotated to tori's right rear to a position with the instep some six to eighteen inches behind the right heel (the distance depending on tori's length of leg and the relative size of his opponent). The left foot is placed at right angles to the right, and thus is pointed slightly away from uke, *i.e.,* to tori's left. (Fig. 57).

As the feet move, tori's body rotates somewhat in a counterclockwise direction, the right hip and tanden going forward close to uke's body and producing an almost straight line from the right foot up the

103

Fig. 56. KOUCHIGARI I. The initial action.

Fig. 57. KOUCHIGARI I. Placement of the feet and body.

leg and side. This position is essential since the power of the sweeping leg is proportionately reduced to the degree that it is compelled to reach out in front of the body to strike. As the left foot comes into position, considerable weight must be transferred to it in order that the right foot may be free to commence the sweep. However, care must be taken that this transfer is confined to the weight alone, and does not cause the body to be withdrawn from its stance close to uke.

From the position thus reached, tori performs the reaping action with the right foot from which the technique derives its name. Among the numerous ways in which this can be done, the following form appears to be by far the most effective.

The right foot is turned so that the little toe is down and the sole of the foot vertical, facing to tori's left. In this position the foot and leg sweep strongly against uke's right leg. The arch of the foot strikes the inside of uke's right ankle and drives it *outward*, that is, to uke's right (Fig. 58). The impact must be sharp and vigorous but is not a mere kick. The foot must "follow through" much in the manner of ashiharai, sweeping low along the mat and forcing uke's foot outward until it can no longer retain contact with the mat. With diligent practice, tori can learn to take control of uke's ankle almost as if the instep of the sweeping foot were the palm of a hand. This degree of skill makes the technique extremely difficult to avoid, even though the physical impact against uke's ankle is relatively mild.

Fig. 58. KOUCHIGARI I. The throw in progress.

This form of sweeping is preferable to that usually described in which the foot is swept to tori's rear, for two reasons. First of all, any action in which a leg reaches out and then exerts force in a backward pull tends to limit the source of power to the muscles of the leg alone. Even when tori's body and hip are well forward at the time the sweep commences, this weakness is present to some degree. The outward sweep, on the other hand, makes it easier to derive power from the hips and abdomen. Second, a sweep directly to the rear is likely to miss uke's leg entirely, and pass inside it without making contact. A sweep outward is easier to control and affords a better target.

It is likewise preferable to the form in which tori hooks his heel behind uke's ankle. Passable skill in the use of the heel can be acquired with considerably less effort than is required to master the foot sweep. However, it precludes any attempt to drive uke's foot outward rather than to the rear, and, at best, lacks the subtlety and potential for full control of uke's body found in the recommended method.

Simultaneously with the foot sweep, tori's left hand continues its vigorous downward pull on uke's right sleeve. The right hand drives downward and to uke's right rear. Tori's body continues to move forward, led by the lowered right shoulder and right side. His head drops sharply to his chest and moves toward uke's right rear (Fig. 58). Care must be taken that the right hand does not move to uke's left, directly to his rear, or upward in the manner appropriate to osoto-gari.

Fig. 59. KOUCHIGARI II. An alternate method of placing the right foot and head.

As a result of this action, uke's balance is broken and his whole weight moved to a position of dependence on his right leg. However, since this leg has been swept out by tori's right foot, uke is forced to fall, striking the mat to his right rear.

Kouchigari II

The following variant of kouchigari, while no more effective than the classical form, is considerably more violent and may be useful in shiai. It is particularly suitable against opponents who contest in a jigotai position with the upper body forward and the arms stiff.

The initial movements are the same as in the classical form. However, tsukuri is strongly downward with both hands as if seeking to pull uke's upper body toward the mat. Sometimes a rocking action, in which tori first pushes forward before drawing uke strongly downward, will be effective here. As he pulls downward, tori lowers his head and shoulders, placing his head on the outside of uke's right arm with his right cheek against the bicep (Fig. 59). His body turns in the usual way, but the knees are somewhat more bent, and he seeks to achieve a complete contact between his right hip, side, and shoulder, and the body of uke.

In this technique, tori's right heel is hooked behind uke's right ankle. Kake is performed by sweeping uke's foot strongly to tori's rear. Tori's left hand pulls downward, his head drops on his chest, and his whole body follows the right hand in a violent surge in the

Fig. 60. KOUCHIGARI III. Drawing uke forward.   Fig. 61. KOUCHIGARI III. The throw in progress.

direction of uke's right rear. As tori's upper body moves forward over his foot which reaps in the opposite direction, uke will be driven violently to the mat, and tori will frequently go down with him. It should be noted that, despite its considerable variance from the classical form of kouchigari, this method still requires that uke's leg be taken near the ankle. It should not be hooked up near the knee as in ouchigari.

Kouchigari III

A third variation of kouchigari is unique in that tori, in the initial stages of the throw, is moving backward rather than forward.

The form is initiated when tori has withdrawn his left foot and uke follows by advancing his right foot. At the moment when uke's right foot is about to settle on the mat and his weight is moving forward onto it, tori, with both hands on the lapels, pulls them strongly downward, forward, and then upward in a circular motion. The effect of the downward and forward pull is to draw uke's body forward, breaking his balance and fixing his weight on his advanced right foot (Fig. 60). At the same time tori transfers his own weight to his left foot and bends the knee slightly. He then advances his right foot and engages the back of uke's right ankle, sweeping it strongly to uke's front. At the same time tori's hands complete their circular action, moving powerfully upward and forward against uke's chest (Fig. 61). This movement is supported by a forward movement of tori's shoulders and chest, deriving power from the expansion of his whole body. His head drops sharply to his chest as kake is performed. Uke's upper body is driven backward as the leg upon which his weight has been fixed is reaped forward, and he is thrown to the mat.

While this form obviously does not employ as much of tori's available power as the more orthodox methods, prospects of success with it are enhanced because uke will not be accustomed to being attacked in this fashion while moving toward his opponent.

Although most suited to kouchigari, these same principles *(i.e.,* the preparation for attack while tori is moving backward; the circular action of the hands; and the attack directly to uke's rear) may also be employed in ouchigari and kosotogari. They may be particularly useful in providing a versatile and well-rounded attack for judoka who prefer to contest with both hands at the lapels rather than in the usual style with one hand at the sleeve.

12

Kouchisutemi

Kouchisutemi is a sacrifice throw derived from the regular form of kouchigari. In this technique, the initial action is similar to kouchigari—the right foot is advanced; the left foot rotated to a position behind it; and uke's weight is fixed on his right foot by a downward pull on his right sleeve and a push downward and to his right rear on the lapel.

At this point, however, tori releases the grip of the right hand and drives his body vigorously downward and to his left. His head is placed beside uke's right thigh and his shoulder and right side are brought against uke's right thigh and waist. Tori's right arm reaches forward and downward along the back of uke's right leg and his right hand grasps the back of uke's calf (Fig. 62). The movement must be carried out with speed and vigor. Care must be taken that the forward impetus of the body is not lost when the weight is removed from the right foot in order to permit it to be lifted for a sweep.

As he takes a grip on uke's right leg, tori lifts his own right foot and, with the right heel, hooks the back of uke's right leg low down on the calf. As this foot drives uke's right leg toward tori's rear, tori's body continues to drive violently forward and downward. His body rotates in a counterclockwise direction, presenting the back of his right shoulder to the front of his opponent.

As a consequence of this action, uke's right leg is driven toward his front or, at least, is held motionless. As tori's right shoulder and back force the upper part of uke's body to the rear, he is upset and driven violently to the mat under tori's falling body.

While kouchisutemi is an extremely virile throw and of considerable value in contest, one must go "all out" in order to succeed with it.

Fig. 62. KOUCHISUTEMI. Initial position of the body, right hand, and feet.

Any indecision or hesitation is particularly dangerous since, if kouchi-sutemi is not brought off, it leaves the judoka who attempts it partic-ularly open to retaliation, especially if his opponent is skilled in newaza. If an attempt at kouchisutemi misses or results only in waza-ari, uke is placed in an ideal position to apply shimewaza.

An interesting variation of this orthodox technique may be noted. As tori drives forward in the attack, he may rotate his body in a counterclockwise direction, drawing his left shoulder well around, turning his head sharply to his left, and presenting his whole back to his opponent. This form widens the area of impact and is extremely effective. Its only defect is that it places tori in an even more danger-ous position to be strangled if he does not bring the trick off success-fully.

13

Ashiharai

The movements of ashiharai are relatively less complex than those of many other forms. Success in its use is dependent more upon the selection of the proper time in the course of the opponent's movements to make the attempt. We will therefore first describe the movement itself (as an attack by the left leg against the opponent's right leg) and then consider when it should be employed.

To commence, the weight must be well balanced upon the right foot with the right knee slightly bent. The toes of the right foot should point somewhat outward: *i.e.*, toward tori's right. If this is not done, (that is, if tori's foot points directly toward uke and at right angles to the path of the proposed sweep), his whole right hip and side will be frozen in place and a smooth powerful sweep will become impossible. It is a universal principle for all ashiwaza that the toes of the "platform" foot *must* be pointed in the direction toward which the sweep is to be made.

With the left toe pointed and the foot turned inward (that is, with the outer edge of the foot toward the ground and the sole of the foot almost vertical) tori then sweeps the leg strongly to his right (Fig. 63). Tori's instep strikes uke's right leg just at the ankle. The sweeping foot continues to the right, remaining close to the ground as long as possible with the little toe touching the mat, or nearly so. As the foot sweeps, the leg is straightened and the left hip and tanden freely follow the action of the leg. The tanden must remain forward throughout the sweep (Fig. 64).

Simultaneously with the sweeping action, tori's left hand draws strongly downward on uke's right sleeve. Tori's right hand assists the action by drawing the left side of uke's body upward and across to his

Fig. 63. ASHIHARAI. The initial position.

right. The hand movement may be visualized most effectively by considering uke's body as if it were a large wheel, set vertically and facing the front. Tori's hands act as if they were rotating such a wheel in a counterclockwise direction, the left hand pulling downward on one side of the rim while the right hand lifts the other. Tori's shoulders and upper body give way slightly to his left, countering the action of the left hip and leg, while his chin drops to his chest as the left hand pulls downward. The foot remains in close contact with uke's right ankle, sweeping it across in front of his body. Uke, deprived of the support of this foot, is pulled to the mat directly in front of tori (Fig. 65). Care must be taken that the action of the foot is a true sweep and that it is completed with a firm "follow through." A spasmodic kick, no matter how violent, will be less likely to succeed. In this form, as well as in all other ashiwaza techniques, particular care must be taken that the right or "platform" foot remains flat on the ground at all times. Tori's body balance will be impaired and the power of his hand action seriously reduced if this foot is permitted to come up on the toes.

Ashiharai may be more accurately called deashiharai, which is translated as "advanced foot sweep." There are two situations in which this form should be employed.

It may be used against the opponent's advancing right foot, just as that foot reaches the ground. In this case, tori will withdraw his own right foot as uke advances his left. Tori's right foot may well be moved a little farther to the rear and the right than would ordinarily be the

Fig. 64. ASHIHARAI. Commencing the sweep.

Fig. 65. ASHIHARAI. The sweep in progress.

case in order to establish a firm foundation for the sweep. A slight outward pull of tori's right hand may induce uke to react in the direction of his own right as he advances his right foot. The sweep should take uke's right foot just as his weight 's about to be transferred to it. To achieve this result, his action must anticipate uke's move and commence just as uke starts to advance his right foot. If this is not done, the contact will probably not be made until uke's weight has become well established on his right foot and the sweep will be ineffectual.

Once tori has commenced to withdraw his left foot to the rear, he will find it difficult to change its direction of movement in time to sweep uke's foot. Most judoka will find it helpful if, having withdrawn the right foot, the left foot hesitates for an instant in its original position and then sweeps directly to the right. The sweep may thus be timed to the same rhythm as that of uke's right foot in its normal advance—thereby increasing tori's chance of engaging his opponent's ankle at the right moment.

Ashiharai II

The second, and probably most effective, form of ashiharai is taken as opponent retreats. In this style, tori will press forward against uke's chest with the right hand, thereby inducing uke to withdraw his left foot. Tori advances his own right foot correspondingly, moving just a

Ashiharai **113**

shade faster than usual and to a position slightly wider to his right than normal. The sweep is commenced in time to take uke's right ankle just as the weight is leaving the foot but not so late as to permit uke to withdraw it readily and escape the attack. Because tori is moving forward, his sweep will usually have added impetus. Thus it should be more effective than the first style mentioned in which the sweep depends on a movement directly across the line in which tori's body is moving, rather than one more in the same direction.

It will be observed that in ashiharai the crucial factor is to move at the right time in relation to the movement of the opponent. The action of the hands is not employed to break the opponent's balance in the same sense as in a koshiwaza technique where a strong initial tsukuri is used to force uke into a weakened posture. The *initial* hand action here is employed rather to guide uke's natural movements into a position from which the sweep can be applied. A vigorous hand action is, of course, required in kake if the throw is to be successfully completed.

In practicing the second form of ashiharai described above, it will be found that uke's right foot is sometimes swept across in front of his left while at other times it is brought up against his left ankle. In the latter case, the throw will bear a close outward resemblance to okuri-ashiharai. However, there is a clear mechanical distinction between the two. In ashiharai, the pull is primarily downward, drawing uke to the ground over the point from which his right foot has been removed. In okuriashiharai, however, uke's whole body is drawn upward, and is allowed to fall only after both feet are swept from the ground.

14

Okuriashiharai

Okuriashiharai is regarded by many experts as the quintessence of pure judo. While appearing on casual inspection to be quite simple, it requires the most delicate sense of timing. Of all the techniques in the judo repertoire, it is perhaps the most difficult to "force" by the employment of mere physical strength. Even the most highly skilled judoka cannot hope to achieve a perfect result with every effort.

The action of the foot in okuriashiharai is quite similar to that of ashiharai insofar as tori is concerned. The primary difference in the two forms resides in the state of uke's balance at the time of the attack. The name okuriashiharai, which is translated as "sliding foot sweep" indicates the nature of this difference.

In okuriashiharai, tori takes a full grip of the cloth of uke's jacket, with both hands placed out toward the armpits rather than on the collar itself. As uke moves his left foot to the side, tori follows this action with his right foot which advances in a corresponding direction with the knee bent and the toe turned slightly outward, that is, to tori's right (Fig. 66). It is desirable that tori move slightly wider with this foot than might be the case if no attack were to be attempted. At this time, tori exerts a slight pressure with his right hand against uke's left nipple, thereby encouraging uke to withdraw his left foot and perhaps to react slightly forward with his upper body. As he advances the right foot, tori must be sure that his tanden remains well forward.

As uke then withdraws his right foot toward his left, tori sweeps this foot in the direction it is already moving with an action similar to that employed in ashiharai (Fig. 67). Care must be taken that the contact is made with the sole of the foot and that the sweep is made close to the ground. The action is definitely a sweeping and not a striking one

Fig. 66. OKURIASHIHARAI. Preparing for the attack.

Fig. 67. OKURIASHIHARAI. Commencing the sweep.

—the ultimate stage of perfection would be for tori to use this foot as a hand, grasping uke's right ankle with the sole of his foot and carrying it at an accelerated pace along the mat toward uke's left foot.

Success with this depends ultimately upon moving uke's left foot, rather than his right, so this is the point to be aimed at. Provided that the sole of tori's foot makes a strong and clean contact at this point, slight inaccuracies in meeting uke's right foot are not crucial. Sometimes tori's foot will pass behind uke's right foot and make the initial contact here with the lower calf.

Simultaneously with the sweep of the foot, tori pulls *hard* with both hands executing a small circular movement and drawing uke's body upward. This action is extremely difficult to describe in words. It resembles an inverted figure six, thus, ∂, with the loop of the six placed parallel to uke's body, and the tail extending upward and over tori's left shoulder. The action is as if tori were seeking to rip uke's jacket violently off over his head, and cast it backward over tori's left shoulder.

As the hands pull, tori's shoulders draw backward and to the left, countering the action of his hips and tanden which follow his foot sweep and straightened leg in the same manner as in ashiharai. Indeed, the extension of tori's leg and the advance of his abdomen is even more pronounced since the upward tsukuri and shoulder movement

Fig. 68. OKURIASHIHARAI. Completing the throw, with uke in full flight and tori's left foot already returning to the ground.

furnish a more favorable counterbalance for the sweep than the downward pull of ashiharai. Tori's chin drops to his chest as the hands pull upward and the foot sweeps.

If this technique is performed correctly, tori's left foot carries uke's sliding right foot back into his left and sweeps both feet off the mat. This action, combined with the continuing pull of the hands, rotates uke's body in a counterclockwise direction and lifts it into the air (Fig. 68). Ideally, uke's body will assume an almost horizontal position with its back down and, being totally unsupported, will fall to the mat immediately in front of tori.

It will be readily understood that this extreme displacement of uke's body, produced by a relatively mild physical effort, will follow only if every element is perfectly coordinated. The movement of both hands and feet by tori must occur at the precisely correct time in relation to each other and to the withdrawal of uke's right foot. This sense of timing is almost impossible to define in words, and can be acquired only by long and diligent practice.

15

Tsurikomiashi

Tsurikomiashi, like its related form, hizaguruma, is distinguished from other ashiwaza in that tori's foot does not move against uke, but serves as a prop or fulcrum over which his body is drawn.

The throw may be done with the usual grip, but is probably more effective if both hands are placed on uke's jacket at the lapels, or outside of them near the armpits. As uke advances his right foot, tori pulls strongly on his right lapel, drawing uke's weight forward onto the advanced right foot (Fig. 69). Before uke has an opportunity to advance his left foot to regain his balance, tori advances his own right foot, placing it (with the toes pointed to the left) to the left of and just outside the line of uke's left foot.

Simultaneously, tori pulls strongly a second time with his left hand. His whole body is rotated in a counterclockwise direction with his chest well opened and his left shoulder drawn vigorously backward, thereby producing a continuous pull with the left hand in a circular path (Fig. 70). His right hand presses against uke's chest, moving the latter's body in a circular direction to its own right. The hands act as if uke's shoulder girdle was a spoke of a wheel which was being revolved in a counterclockwise circle. During this movement, tori's weight is fixed on his right foot; his tanden remains forward, and his hips rotate like the shoulders with the left hip drawn back. His chin turns slightly to the left and drops toward the left pectoral muscle. Care must be taken that the right hand does not force uke's left shoulder directly to his rear, since this will tend to restore his balance, and destroy tori's control of the movement. The force of the right hand is exerted upward and to tori's left, thus insuring that uke's

Fig. 69. TSURIKOMIASHI. The initial tsukuri.

Fig. 70. TSURIKOMIASHI. The throw in progress.

body rotates rather than moving backward. In the final stages of the throw, this hand will actually draw uke forward over tori's foot.

As tori executes these movements, he extends his left foot with the leg straight, the toes pointed, the outer edge of the foot toward the ground, and the sole of the foot toward the front. This foot is moved to a position close to the mat and directly in front of uke's right ankle. Care must be taken that tori does not overreach with this foot in an attempt to sweep uke's ankle, or make a contact too far to his own front. His left leg and foot provide a fulcrum over which uke is to be drawn, but, for practical purposes, are held still at the time contact is made.

The pull of tori's hands continues in a circular path, just as if they were turning a large horizontal wheel. As a result of this action, uke is drawn forward until the right ankle engages the sole of tori's left foot (Fig. 70). As his ankle is intercepted in this position, uke's body continues to rotate and move forward. Tori's left hand, which has been leading the movement, now pulls strongly downward. The strength of this action will be increased if the arm is bent and the left elbow is drawn down to or past tori's left hip. Uke's body is thus whirled around and over his propped ankle, and dropped to the ground just to tori's left.

It will be observed that this form tends to draw uke into the movement which is required for its successful execution and can be em-

Fig. 71. SASAE-TSURIKOMIASHI. The initial body and leg contact.

ployed against an opponent who is relatively well stabilized. However, variations are available for use in other circumstances.

An opponent who stands block still in a defensive posture with his tanden well forward may sometimes be led into this throw if both hands pull strongly downward (the left hand being somewhat accentuated), thus inducing him to advance his right foot to regain balance.

An opponent who moves loosely and relies on agility for defense may be attacked in a different fashion. Tori anticipates the advance of uke's right foot, and, just as it is about to occur, springs into position with his right foot well to the outside of uke's left, and his whole body moved to that side. The technique is performed from that point with a similar hand and foot action. This is, except for the lower position of the foot, identical with hizaguruma, under which heading it is described in greater detail.

Sasae-tsurikomiashi

An extremely virile variant of this form is that accurately designated as sasae-tsurikomiashi. It is commenced with tori's right hand on the lapel and his left hand usually on the sleeve. Tori first advances his right foot with the toe turned to his left, to a position inside of and next to uke's left foot. The outer side of tori's calf and thigh are moved against the inside of uke's left calf and thigh, driving uke's left leg to his left rear (Fig. 71). Since tori's foot remains on the

Tsurikomigoshi   **121**

Fig. 72. SASAE-TSURIKOMIASHI. The start of the throw.

ground at this point, uke's leg is not lifted from the mat or violently displaced as in hanegoshi or uchimata, but the impact tends to loosen the contact of this foot with the ground and compels uke to shift his weight onto his right foot. Tori assumes a close body-to-body position. His tanden is, in effect, inserted under that of uke, and exerts a lifting force, supplementing the action of the hands with the power of tori's whole body.

Simultaneously with this movement, tori's right hand executes a lift-pull very much in the manner of tsurikomigoshi, lifting uke's body upward and forward (Fig. 72). Tori's left hand pulls uke's right arm upward and outward in a circular path. Tori's left shoulder is withdrawn, leading his whole upper body in a circular counterclockwise motion, with the left elbow raised and the chest widely opened. Tori's weight has been transferred to his right foot which serves as a pivot around which his body rotates. As his chest and shoulders are opened, his tanden remains forward behind the extended left leg. His chin turns slightly to his left and drops into position just below his left shoulder.

The effect of this action by the hands is to remove uke's weight almost entirely from his left foot and transfer it to the toes, (and particularly the little toe) of his right foot. The pull forces his right arm to full extension forward, and his balance is broken upward and to his right front.

As tori executes this move, he extends his left foot in the same manner as the orthodox style. The hands continue the pull with the left hand raised shoulder high and the right hand drawing uke forward and pressing him to his right. Uke is whirled over his propped right ankle and thrown to the mat.

If tori prefers to place both hands on the lapels, the left hand will join the right in the initial upward and forward pull. In this event the emphasis on *upward* displacement of uke's balance is increased and the body action is even more pronounced. The left hand then draws forward and finally downward on the lapel, the action of this hand being similar to that employed in the usual form of tsurikomiashi heretofore described.

Sasae-tsurikomiashi may be more effective than the ordinary method for three reasons: First, the impact against uke's left leg makes it somewhat more forceful; second, the vigorous lifting action of the body aids in destroying uke's balance more effectively than may be done with the hands alone; and third, the point at which tori's foot blocks uke's ankle is closer to uke's original position, thereby giving him less opportunity to step over or otherwise avoid it. However, it has two corresponding disadvantages: First, the close-in position and contact against uke's leg is difficult to achieve; and second, if the contact of leg and body is not properly made so that uke's left leg and hip are neutralized, tori lays himself open to an extremely heavy counter, probably with kosotogari. Therefore, it may be wise not to attempt this method until it has been perfected by long practice.

16

Hizaguruma

Hizaguruma is identical in principle with tsurikomiashi—involving the same rotary action of the hands, the withdrawal of tori's body, and the use of his foot as a fulcrum. The sole difference between the two forms arises from a different placement of the feet.

In hizaguruma, tori's right foot is moved to a position in front of and to the outside of uke's left foot, the precise distance depending on tori's length of arm and leg (Fig. 73). The toes are turned to the left, with the foot almost parallel with a line drawn between uke's feet. This position of the feet makes possible, and, indeed compels, the rotation of tori's body and the forward position of his right hip and tanden already noted in tsurikomiashi. For maximum effectiveness, tori will leap into this position, combining foot, body, and hand action in a single effort.

As tori's body moves, his left foot will be raised until the sole of the foot is in a position immediately in front of uke's left knee. Uke is drawn forward until the knee is intercepted by this raised foot, and is then whirled over it to the mat (Fig. 74). Because of the altered position of the feet, it is necessary that tori's body be somewhat lower, and his arms somewhat more raised and extended than in tsurikomiashi.

Because of the width of the movement and the lack of a vigorous body impact, this form is probably less desirable against an opponent who remains in a strong upright defensive position, but may be extremely effective against one whose natural style is mobile.

Fig. 73. HIZAGURUMA. Tori's movement to the side.

Fig. 74. HIZAGURUMA. The throw in progress.

Hizaguruma II

A relatively short judoka may sometimes vary this form in a manner which combines elements of hizaguruma and sasae-tsurikomiashi. Tori will drop low by bending his knees, and move close to his opponent. His right foot is not so far to uke's left but is placed more in front of the latter's left foot or even close in against his left leg as in sasae-tsurikomiashi. In the initial stages of the throw, the upward displacement of uke's body is emphasized, and tori must employ the strength of his expanding body as well as that of his hands (Fig. 75). When the close-in position is achieved and uke has been unbalanced, tori's right hand continues to draw uke upward and to his right front, while the left hand pulls strongly downward. This turns uke over the fulcrum formed by tori's left foot, and drops him to the mat somewhat closer to his original position than with the usual style. Tori may place his left foot at any point between uke's ankle and knee which feels most comfortable.

Fig. 75. HIZAGURUMA II. A variant method performed from a close-in position.

This form requires exceptional strength, and the ability to exert it
explosively within a rather restricted body position. However, one
whose physique permits will find it useful, especially against a taller
opponent who maintains a strong and rather static upright defensive
posture.

17

Recapitulation

Despite much popular nonsense which is frequently heard on the subject, there are no magic formulas in judo. Long and diligent practice is more important in achieving success than the adoption of any particular system. Indeed, the use of the word "system" may be somewhat misleading in itself because there are actually more similarities than differences in the way in which any two competent judoka will perform the same technique. However, each experienced practitioner of the art is sure to develop a personal opinion as to which particular items among the many points involved in each technique contributes the most to a successful outcome. These patterns of emphasis in thinking or teaching will constitute each individual "system."

The principles of physics and mechanics apply to any activity which involves the movement of physical objects. The degree of ease with which any machine operates and the relation it achieves between power input and result is directly proportionate to its observance of these principles. In this respect a judo throw is no different from any other mechanical operation. The more closely the features which are selected for emphasis coincide with the relevant principles of mechanics, the more efficient the resulting process will be.

The word "efficient" is used advisedly in this connection. Its dictionary definition, in a mechanical context is "The ratio of energy or work that is got out of a machine to the energy put in." The outcome of an attempt at a throw in a particular match between two particular opponents may depend on an infinite number of factors, such as the relative size, strength, speed, experience, and fighting spirit of the contestants. However, the true measure of a given method of performing judo is not necessarily its success or failure in any single contest. It is rather the ability to produce consistently a maximum result with a minimum expenditure of resources—in other words, its efficiency.

Having now considered a number of forms in detail, it may be helpful to re-examine them as a whole and determine if any operating principles are present which are more or less common to all. If such principles can be isolated, generalized, and thoughtfully employed during practice, better results should follow. The student will learn to make more effective use of his practice time; to distinguish readily between essentials and superficialities; and, if necessary, to reach a more intelligent compromise between the theoretical requirements of good style and his own mental and physical makeup. A careful analysis discloses that the patterns of emphasis followed throughout this text can be reduced to the four basic axioms which follow.

AXIOM I. The efficiency of a given form is proportionate to the degree in which tori's hands *achieve* and *maintain* control of uke's body.

AXIOM II. The efficiency of a given form is proportionate to the degree in which the particular body contact it calls for is *achieved* and *maintained*.

AXIOM III. The power developed in an attempted throw is proportionate to the degree in which tori's lower abdomen remains forward and his chest is expanded.

AXIOM IV. Efficiency in completing a given throw is proportionate to the degree in which tori's hips, and particularly his leading hip, remain low at the time of kake.

Of course these are broad generalized statements, and an appreciation of them cannot substitute for a knowledge of the detailed requirements of each form. Likewise, the relative importance of each axiom may vary from one technique to another. However, they are the essential framework upon which a good judo style can be built. A student who bears them in mind should find that his practice becomes more effective and his rate of progress is substantially enhanced.

Glossary

The purpose of the following glossary is to assist those who find literal translations of Japanese names a useful memory aid, or who may have commenced their study of Judo in a school where only Anglicized terminology is employed. For convenience in comparing them to the translations, many of the Japanese terms defined have been separated into their component parts (although most of them would not normally be written in this way).

ASHI Leg or foot

ASHI HARAI Foot sweep (sometimes pronounced ASHI BARAI)

ASHI WAZA Foot technique

DE ASHI HARAI Advanced foot sweep

ERI SEOI NAGE Collar shoulder throw

GOSHI The hips, waist or loins (also written as KOSHI)

HANE GOSHI Springing hip

HARAI GOSHI Sweeping hip

HIZA GURUMA Knee wheel

IPPON SEOI NAGE One (arm) shoulder throw

IPPON SEOI OTOSHI One (arm) shoulder drop

JUDOKA One who practices judo

KAKE The act of throwing

KO A prefix signifying small or minor

KOSHI The hips, waist, or loins (also written as GOSHI)

KOSHI WAZA Hip technique

KO SOTO GARI Minor outer reaping

KO UCHI GARI Minor inner reaping

KO UCHI SUTEMI Minor inner self-abandonment

MURI Unreasonable (referring to a throw achieved by excessive physical power, despite the lack of correct methods)

NE WAZA Grappling techniques (also referred to as KATAMEWAZA)

O A prefix signifying large or major

O GOSHI Major hip

OKURI ASHI HARAI Sliding foot sweep

O SOTO GAKE Major outer hooking

131

O SOTO GARI Major outer reaping

O SOTO OTOSHI Major outer drop

O UCHI GARI Major inner reaping

RANDORI Free practice of judo (as distinguished from SHIAI, a contest, or KATA, a demonstration of pre-arranged forms)

SAIKA TANDEN Lower abdomen

SASAE TSURI KOMI ASHI Propping lift pull foot

SHIMEWAZA Choking techniques (from *shimeru*, to close)

SEOI NAGE Shoulder throw

SEOI OTOSHI Shoulder drop

SODE O SOTO GARI Sleeve major outer reaping

SODE TSURI KOMI GOSHI Sleeve lift pull hip

TACHI WAZA Standing techniques

TAI OTOSHI Body drop

TANDEN Abdomen

TE WAZA Hand techniques

TORI The person applying a judo technique to an opponent (from *toru*, to put)

TSUKURI The action which breaks an opponent's balance and prepares his body to receive the attack (from *tsukuru*, to make or build)

TSURI KOMI ASHI Lift pull foot

TSURI KOMI GOSHI Lift pull hip

UCHIMATA Inner thigh

UCHI KOMI A method of practice consisting of many continuous repetitions of a given form, carried up to the point of kake but without completing the throw (also referred to as BUTSOKARI)

UKE The person receiving a judo attack (from *ukeru*, to receive)

UKI GOSHI Floating hip

WAZA Trick or technique

WAZA-ARI A half-point, allowed by the referee for a throw not quite clean or rapid enough to justify ending the bout

Index

133